NEEDS ASSESSMENT
ANALYSIS AND PRIORITIZATION

James W. Altschuld | Jeffry L. White

The Ohio State University | *University of Louisiana at Lafayette*

Series Editor: James W. Altschuld

NEEDS ASSESSMENT KIT **4**

Ⓢ SAGE

Los Angeles | London | New Delhi
Singapore | Washington DC

For information:

SAGE Publications, Inc.
2455 Teller Road
Thousand Oaks,
   California 91320
E-mail: order@sagepub.com

SAGE Publications India Pvt. Ltd.
B 1/I 1 Mohan Cooperative
   Industrial Area
Mathura Road, New Delhi 110 044
India

SAGE Publications Ltd.
1 Oliver's Yard
55 City Road
London EC1Y 1SP
United Kingdom

SAGE Publications
   Asia-Pacific Pte. Ltd.
33 Pekin Street #02-01
Far East Square
Singapore 048763

Printed in the United States of America

Library of Congress Cataloging-in-Publication Data

Altschuld, James W.
Needs assessment. Analysis and prioritization (book 4)/James W. Altschuld, Jeffry L. White.
     p. cm.
Includes bibliographical references and index.
ISBN 978-1-4129-7557-5 (pbk.)
   1. Strategic planning. 2. Needs assessment. I. White, Jeffry L., 1954-
II. Title.

HD30.28.A38854 2010
361.2—dc22   2009036267

This book is printed on acid-free paper.

09   10   11   12   13   10 9 8 7 6 5 4 3 2 1

Acquisitions Editor:	Vicki Knight
Associate Editor:	Lauren Habib
Editorial Assistant:	Ashley Dodd
Production Editor:	Brittany Bauhaus
Copy Editor:	Melinda Masson
Typesetter:	C&M Digitals (P) Ltd.
Proofreader:	Victoria Reed-Castro
Indexer:	Diggs Publication Services, Inc.
Cover Designer:	Candice Harman
Marketing Manager:	Stephanie Adams

Brief Contents

Detailed Contents

Preface

At initial glance it may seem that this book does not quite fit with the first one in the KIT, which is an overview of the needs assessment process, and the other three that parallel the phases of assessment. Numerous useful tables are embedded in them, as are ways to analyze and portray the data and information that have been collected. This book may appear to be redundant and a bit of overkill.

There is some overlap, not an undue amount. Our firmly held impression is that the two main topics of this text tend to be glossed over when needs assessments are conducted, prioritization in particular. The senior author never ceases to be amazed when he queries supposedly knowledgeable needs assessors about ways in which needs-based priorities are determined. Usually when this question is brought up in group settings, followed by others involving how one need was selected over another and upon what criteria such decisions were made, a pregnant pause (silence) is noticeable. It seems that the outcomes were sort of decided by an invisible mechanism without well-defined rules or even semiapparent structures to guide choices. For relatively small needs this isn't a problem, but in large organizations with competing needs, the absence of criteria and decision rules can have a serious effect on priorities.

Indeed, one example in Book 1 is about an organization that funded work in an area that did not prove to be in accord with the needs of its clientele. A structured prioritization strategy would have prevented this wasteful expenditure of funds. All of the above observations underscore the perception that a separate book devoted to analysis and prioritization is a valuable addition to the four others in the KIT.

It is our sincere hope that this volume provides a good overview of how to analyze two distinct types of data, pull them together in a meaningful way, and derive priorities from the collation of the information that has been generated by the needs assessment. What should result is a stronger foundation for needs-related decisions and one that will stand the scrutiny of involved and questioning audiences. If that foundation is not there and the priorities are challenged, they are difficult to defend. Having a basis for coming to final decisions is a step forward.

By the same token, it is recognized that data obtained from multiple groups and methods may not fall easily or simply into alignment and even may be contradictory. Therefore, ultimate priorities often result from negotiations with key stakeholders and groups. The text offers guidance rather than absolute solutions to help needs assessment committees (NACs) and their facilitators work through the complexities of analysis and subsequent prioritization.

❖ A FEW NOTES ABOUT CONTENT

The content in the text is an overview of analytic and prioritization procedures and not a comprehensive treatment of all strategies in this regard. If the local circumstances require specialized indices and other aspects of the two processes, seek out sources in the literature.

As indicated in its title this is Book 4 in the Needs Assessment KIT. The other books are:

Book 1: *Needs Assessment: An Overview*

Book 2: *Needs Assessment Phase I: Getting Started*

Book 3: *Needs Assessment Phase II: Collecting Data*

Book 5: *Needs Assessment Phase III: Taking Action for Change*

Acknowledgments

We would like to express our appreciation to Yi-Fang Lee with whom we worked (2003–2005) in a complex evaluation project that utilized surveys with needs types of questions in them. Her research, which is frequently cited, benefited us, and thanks are extended for her diligence and insights into what can happen with data. We would also be remiss if we omitted Belle Ruth Witkin's work of 25 years ago that still resonates and had a significant influence on the current text. We would also like to thank the following reviewers:

Stephanie Brzuzy, *Xavier University*

Valerie Larsen, *University of Virginia*

Kui-Hee Song, *California State University, Chico*

Last, we express gratitude to all others whose endeavors have enriched our understandings of needs.

—James W. Altschuld

—Jeffry L. White

About the Authors

James W. Altschuld, PhD, received his bachelor's and master's degrees in chemistry from Case Western Reserve University and The Ohio State University (OSU), respectively. His doctorate is from the latter institution with an emphasis on educational research and development and sociological methods. He is now professor emeritus in the College of Education and Human Ecology at OSU after 27 years of teaching research techniques and program evaluation. In evaluation, he developed and taught a sequence of courses on theory, needs assessment, and design. He has coauthored three previous books (two on needs assessment and the other on the evaluation of science and technology education), has written many chapters on needs assessment as well as others on evaluation research and issues, and has an extensive list of publications, almost all in the field of evaluation. He has given presentations and done work in five countries outside of the United States. In his career he has been the recipient of local, state, and national honors including the Alva and Gunnar Myrdal Practice Award for contributions to evaluation.

Jeffry L. White, PhD, is assistant professor of educational foundations and leadership at the University of Louisiana at Lafayette. He teaches statistics, quantitative research methods, program evaluation, measurement and assessment. He received his doctorate from The Ohio State University in quantitative research, evaluation, and measurement. He has master's degrees in educational research evaluation, and public policy and management, and health services administration. He is a member of the American Evaluation Association and served as chair, cochair, and program chair of the needs assessment Topical Interest Group. He has published in a diverse set of journals.

1

The Data and Prioritization Mess

What Is the NAC Getting Into?

❖ THE DATA SIDE OF THE EQUATION

When needs assessment data have been collected there are two related acts (analysis and prioritization) that are necessary to get meaningful information and move the process forward. These are the foci of this book. Analysis and prioritization are, at times, treated as one, but from our viewpoint that does not best fit the practice and art of the field. Why is that so, and what would we recommend?

Before answering, data collection in the needs context must be examined. In the KIT there has been a continuous drumbeat about the use of multiple methods (quantitative and qualitative) for understanding what can be complex social, institutional, and/or other types of needs. The theme is constant and transparent. That is appropriate, but as such the skills of the needs assessment committee (NAC) and the individuals facilitating its work could be strained to the limit. Multiple methods are great in theory, but in practice it is often difficult to combine the results from them into a coherent picture of needs.

Among notable problems are:

- Qualitative and quantitative methods may produce different data and information.

- Qualitative methods deal with values, feelings, and perceptions but do not lead directly to discrepancies between the "what is" and "what should be" states; instead discrepancies have to be inferred.

- Given the above there is not a common metric across methods against which to compare results.

- Methods may play rather distinct roles in the analysis process, and in some cases, one method (usually a qualitative one) is employed to determine how to implement a quantitative one (particularly a survey).

- Conversely, one could use a survey followed by interviews and discussion with constituencies as to the meaning of the quantitative results.

- Different methods may be utilized with different groups, and in turn the data and their analysis become more complicated. This has been termed a *between-methods* approach (Altschuld & Witkin, 2000), and it is seen frequently in assessments. An example would be where personal interviews can be advantageous for a certain group when its members are reluctant to complete surveys.

- Needs assessment designs vary as to whether data collected will be complementary or expansive for the understanding of discrepancies.

- A method may be implemented in a slightly altered form as when question order or subtlety in wording is changed for, say, students and faculty. This is a *within-methods* variation (Altschuld & Witkin, 2000).

- Quantitative methods may lead to gaps but not the reasons underlying them.

- Qualitative and quantitative data may be so disparate that they cannot be combined in a realistic way and have to be reported separately.   ·

- Most needs assessors do not have a full range of cross-method skills and experiences and may subconsciously or consciously favor certain methods over others. This can be thought of as methodological bias.

- Once in a while, data may not just disagree but be in radical disagreement.

- Reports incorporating outcomes from multiple methods are harder to summarize, write, and pull together into a meaningful, hard-hitting, culminating document that provides an accurate picture of needs and what the data are telling the NAC and the organization.

- The terms *qualitative* and *quantitative* are labels for categories of methods with many subsets of techniques. Qualitative data refer to comments from open-ended survey questions, personal/group interviews, archival records containing verbal descriptions, information received from focus groups, or other related sources of this type; and quantitative information is data from Likert-scaled surveys, questionnaires, number-oriented records, existing data sets, and so forth.

In needs assessment the data are like a jigsaw puzzle when it comes out of the box (see Figure 1.1). When first opened the pieces are spread out and do not form a coherent picture. From there you determine the sides (the frame) before beginning to put it together. The comparison to needs data is not perfect because you have to create the picture without benefit of the complete puzzle on the box. (Creating the picture is harder but more exciting than re-creating it!)

Thinking about qualitative data in the needs assessment context for a moment demonstrates some of the complexity. For example, one purpose of a focus group interview is to uncover how various constituencies perceive a content area that is to be included in a subsequent survey. When interviewees talk, what kinds of terms and references do they include in their comments? What is behind their thought processes when they use certain terms and phrases? Is there common meaning within and across constituencies? Will alternative forms of questions have to be developed for different groups? Would it be better to vary content depending on the way it is perceived by one group or another? This makes needs assessment more difficult but is often necessary and requires attention.

Figure 1.1 The Needs Assessment Jigsaw Data Puzzle

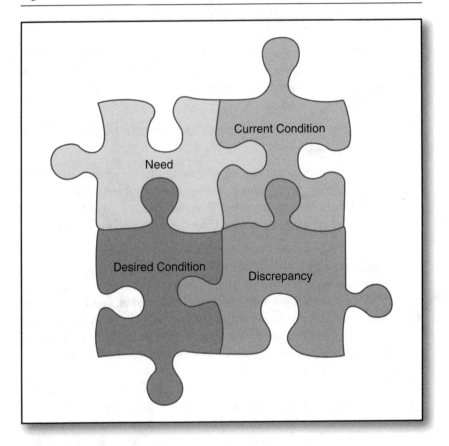

❖ HOW COMPLICATED CAN IT GET?

Consider the case of a questionnaire that dealt partially with percep-tions of technology needs of a representative sample of teachers and administrators in public schools across the country (Altschuld et al., 1997). In the course of constructing the survey, project staff felt they had to tailor questions to the special circumstances of the two groups and the level of school in which they worked. Beyond that it was their perception that it would be beneficial to order the questions differently for the two audiences.

This *within-methods* variation means that similar yet not quite the same instruments were being administered. Could the order have an effect on the results? What about differences in item wording and the possibility of shifts in responses due to it? How are the data from sim-ilar questions to be displayed and compared? This is a very real prob-lem that will be encountered in numerous needs assessment studies.

Four different versions of surveys were developed with relatively similar items in different orders in accord with the audience and school level. The needs assessors developed a concordance sheet (akin to what ministers use for biblical passages) that permitted looking at the results to see how the questions related to each other across forms and as a guide in forming opinions about the comparability or noncomparability of information (see Table 1.1).

Table 1.1 Cross-Instrument Item Concordance Sheet

Question	Form A	Form B	Form C	Form D	Comments
Which of the following resources are available in your classroom, elsewhere in your school, or in your home?	Q.1	Q.2	Question not relevant to respondents	Question not relevant to respondents	Question followed by a list of resources Classroom wording deleted from principal's survey
How do you typically learn about and locate new mathematics and/or science resources for your classroom?	Q.2	Q.2	Q.4 has related content	Q.4 has related content	Question modified for principals with wording like "When you work with teachers . . ."
Rate the following activities and resources in terms of their potential to improve mathematics and/or science education in your classroom and the extent to which they are currently available to you	Q.3	Q.3	Not relevant	Not relevant	Question was followed by a list of resources that might be used by teachers to plan classroom activity Wording modified for principal's form as well as slight modifications in the list of resources
Subsequent survey questions	See above for examples of how to construct entries	See above for examples of how to construct entries	See above for examples of how to construct entries	See above for examples of how to construct entries	See above for examples of how to construct entries

The concerns are twofold. Are the results related enough for purposes of the assessment, and are there meaningful conclusions that can be drawn from the data?

Thinking about pairing quantitative and qualitative evidence, examine the interesting mystery written by Nelson DeMille (2004) titled "Night Fall." In it, the author distinguishes between forensic (quantitative) data and eyewitness (qualitative) testimony as he develops premises and an intricate plot around the troubling crash of TWA Flight 800 in July 1996. The forensic evidence and the official version suggested an internal explosion (probably caused by an electrical short) was the main factor behind the crash—in other words it was an accident, not a terrorist attack. The eyewitness testimony was construed by DeMille to be quite contradictory, and as a result he was able to weave an engaging and "page-turning" storyline.

From fiction to the real world, the same principle applies to needs assessment. We collect data from multiple methods, sources, individuals, and groups. The task is to produce a synthesis taking into account the nature of each source and the degree to which they do or do not converge into a comprehensive and useful understanding of needs.

The NAC has to find ways to collapse the weight of what is many times a surfeit of data into a less dense but more meaningful package that facilitates decision making. Only the most salient aspects of what has been found should be in the condensed version. The task has two components: (a) dealing with data from multiple sources that may or may not agree and (b) finding a presentational format that helps a group make sound choices without burying it in unnecessary and distracting detail.

It's a balancing act worthy of the creativity of an author of fiction, but it is not fiction. Pulling together the data in a way that reduces a large number of needs to a smaller set and culling out the most likely ones for action are an indication that we have accomplished a lot. Prioritization, while not simple, becomes easier when there is a narrower focus.

In Figure 1.2, the idea of taking a large amount of data from multiple sources and funneling it into a more limited set of needs for further consideration is provided. From there the NAC and the decision-making groups within the organization establish priorities for next steps and organizational actions.

Figure 1.2 Summarized Data and Needs Funneling Into Priorities

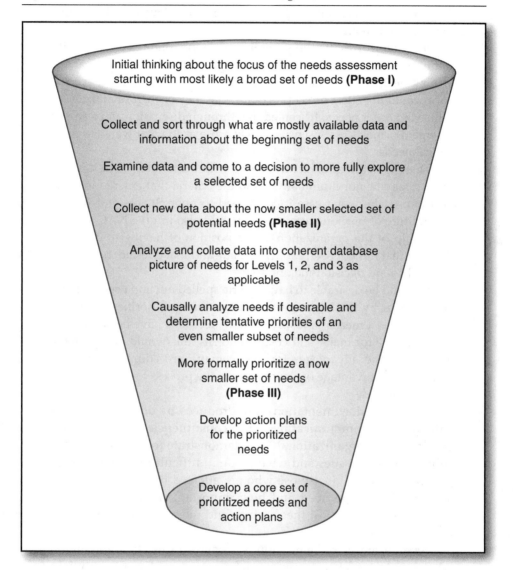

Initial thinking about the focus of the needs assessment starting with most likely a broad set of needs **(Phase I)**

Collect and sort through what are mostly available data and information about the beginning set of needs

Examine data and come to a decision to more fully explore a selected set of needs

Collect new data about the now smaller selected set of potential needs **(Phase II)**

Analyze and collate data into coherent database picture of needs for Levels 1, 2, and 3 as applicable

Causally analyze needs if desirable and determine tentative priorities of an even smaller subset of needs

More formally prioritize a now smaller set of needs **(Phase III)**

Develop action plans for the prioritized needs

Develop a core set of prioritized needs and action plans

❖ PRIORITY SETTING: THE OTHER SIDE OF THINGS

Priorities have to be determined to arrive at needs-based directions for the organization and the wise use of resources. When too many major needs have been uncovered, attending to all would dissipate interest and rapidly dilute resources. So there has to be a way to assign priority scores to needs against agreed-upon criteria relevant to the actions that may be taken.

It is noteworthy that in several workshops conducted on priority setting, one of the authors observed a consistent and disturbing pattern of how decisions are made by professional evaluators. Most participants could not cite a direct procedure that they or their organizations utilized to order needs. It seemed that through discussion and a sort of emergent osmosis, a consensus slowly arose as to what were the most critical needs.

There is nothing inherently wrong with that strategy, but it is neither systematic nor illuminative as to the criteria that entered into the decision. In the worst case it could lead to poor choices and wasted expenditure of precious resources. It would also put the NAC and the leadership of the organization in the position of having to defend a decision that has not been explicitly made and that does not have a formal and sound decision-making trail.

It would be desirable to have criteria spelled out and used in a reliable manner by the NAC or others to determine priorities. Certainly this provides a means of justifying how decisions have been made. If the needs are for major and costly concerns, this would be extremely important. The advantages for a systematic procedure greatly outweigh the disadvantage of slowing down the process to make sure it is on solid ground.

The audit (documentation) trail produced by doing this will be valuable for communicating with constituencies, internal and external to the organization. It will demonstrate to stakeholders the subtle nature of issues and what made it difficult to decide. It isn't just money; it isn't just those who are affected by the need; it isn't just the size of the need and how important the need is for the organization—it's all of these things and more that affect the final course of action.

As an example of being more systematic rather than relying on what was termed before *osmosis*, let's consider what a county in a populous state did. Generally it had made some of its child welfare decisions in an amorphous manner. When it realized that there would be a significant surplus in its budget for the following year (D. Theiss, personal communication, November 6, 2005), it became more attentive to how it should be prioritized. Mindful of potential criticism, the county initiated a well-thought-out needs assessment process with a focus on criteria for selecting future activities. The agencies in the child welfare department were encouraged to maintain a record of what led to their priorities as a way to avoid the possible "heat" that might arise if they followed their previous way of doing things.

So what are possible criteria? Sork (1998) identified two sets (importance and feasibility) that could be employed (see Book 1). In 2000, Altschuld and Witkin added risk as a category to Sork's dichotomy and divided it into risks internal to the organization and those outside its aegis or control. Others see risk in terms of prevalence and incidence (studies of the spread of disease) or look to research to inform future directions such as in regard to the recidivism of sex offenders and pedophiles. Note that whether determined by ratings or by research, all estimates of risk have error inherent in them.

Risk can additionally be assessed via causal analysis in two distinct ways. The first is to determine the most likely causes of needs, especially those that the organization can deal with and those for which it has less ability to change or modify. The second approach is to look at potential solutions to needs-based problems to see where they most likely fail. Both are done routinely in engineering but less so in education and social services, and if carried out in these fields the procedure may predict the failure of some educational programs.

Further, in prioritization the *counterfactual state* must be considered. It is an estimate of what can happen if we did nothing about the need. Recall what transpired when New York City transportation workers went on strike, crippling the country's largest urban center. Fortunately, the strike was short-lived, but it was interesting and even amazing to see how the city and its citizens coped. People began walking or bicycling to work, creating pedestrian traffic jams across some bridges into the city. Police and transportation authorities limited automobiles to those with multiple riders in them. Companies began to rent buses and vans to get employees to work, thus exhausting the supply of such vehicles in short order. Car pools were formed and so forth.

The counterfactual state was that substitute forms of transportation were sought and employed to ameliorate the effects of the strike and the diminished capacity of New Yorkers to go about their work and daily tasks. This was a short-term reflection of a counterfactual state.

For this situation, it was obvious that these alternatives only worked so well. It was taking an excess of time for workers to get to their jobs and return home at the end of the day. If they walked or traveled by other self-propelled means, they probably were more tired and grumpier on the job (but perhaps in better physical shape if the strike had lasted an extended period). As the novelty wore off, it is likely that most individuals were not pleased with ersatz solutions. Business suffered, and sales at the height of the holiday season were seriously impacted. In other words, the counterfactual state had negative consequences.

The strike was settled after a few days, so the discomfort is nothing more than a faded memory. Had it lasted, a unique opportunity would have existed to study the counterfactual state over a long span of time and in relation to the accommodations that individuals and groups made. Many times we do not have the latter type of information.

In this vein, Anderson, Jesswein, and Fleischman (1990) reported that some social needs found in Duluth, Minnesota, were only short-lived in that community members, Level 1 service recipients, found solutions to the underlying problems, thus mitigating their effects. In survey responses, it was notable that respondents gave lower ratings to the needs compared to higher ones given by service providers (Level 2) who may not have been aware of how the problems were being resolved. It simply was not in their range finders, and knowledge of the counterfactual state helped explain the conflicting survey results coming from the Level 1 and 2 constituencies.

Returning to criteria for establishing priorities, in Table 1.2 some general features are given along with authors who propose their use. It goes without saying that each needs assessment is unique to its local context. Criteria should be chosen in accord with specific decisions to be made and sensitivity to how staff and others operate. Take into account what seems to be important to the organization and keep in mind the consequences of attending to or not attending to needs.

Sometimes needs are relatively easy to deal with and won't require much deliberation as in the social ones of a small retirement community. Others like the recreational needs of a small city are more involved and necessitate serious reflection in relation to multifaceted criteria and the different groups that would benefit from improvements. Suppose a new recreation center (workout facilities, pools, meeting rooms, social rooms, etc.) were to be constructed; the question immediately comes up as to where it should be situated, how that location would be perceived, and how it could affect the ultimate use of the facilities.

Table 1.2 General Features of Some Criteria for Prioritizing Needs

Author	Criteria	Comments
Sork (1998)	Importance Size of discrepancy Number affected Requires immediate attention Contribution to organization Instrumental value Feasibility Educational efficacy Resources Commitment to change	Excellent criteria for thinking about the importance of resolving a need and the nature and strength of the organizational orientation to and willingness to commit to the endeavor Involved procedure for the NAC and/or others to rate each need on 8 separate criteria and arrive at priorities
Altschuld & Witkin (2000)	Risk factors such as short- and long-term economic risk, political risks, internal disruption, and others These are divided into internal and external categories	The authors specify 14 risks prior to resources being allocated Use of them in conjunction with Sork's (1998) categories complicates the process Kaufman (1983) posed a simple question: What are the risks associated with deciding not to deal with a need?
Fiorentine (1993, 1999)	Focus on strategies of distributing resources for needs (whether resources should be distributed toward one group with the greatest need or more across groups in regard to political concerns)	The distribution of resources deals with a form of political risk Discussion of alternatives as to how resources can be given out and the consequences of each strategy
Other authors: Kaufman & Cooper (1999); Sampson, Laub, & Wimer (2006)	Studies of counterfactual states such as those dealing in epidemiology and recidivism	Excellent input for prioritization and probably underutilized in terms of education and social programs

❖ AN ORIENTATION TO ANALYSIS AND PRIORITIZATION

There is a lot to think about as the NAC analyzes data, determines priorities, and makes recommendations to the organization. In some cases, there isn't much to do—data are not particularly complex and just come from one group or method. Decisions aren't tough, and the group quickly comes to consensus and moves forward. On the other hand, data in a complex needs project are generally from a variety of groups and information-rich methods. Analysis may not always be straightforward. The integration of multiple data sources (people and instruments) is neither direct nor easily accomplished.

In concert with such data is that prioritization will be important especially when jobs, providing services to families and individuals, distribution of resources, and so forth are on the line. Coming to final decisions requires deliberation through multiple lenses. Needs assessment is a practical exercise that impacts how organizations go about their business and deliver their programs and products to service recipients.

In this more complicated scenario, the process could mire down, and the data could become too much. There are many criteria to think about, and the whole thing is mind-boggling. This is plausible and tends to reflect reality more than we care to admit. (In Book 1 of this KIT the point was made that many needs assessments have neither been published nor evaluated. One reason postulated for this is that they have been less successful than desired.)

The facilitator and the NAC must have a way to work in the more complex situation. From the very first meetings of the NAC, emphasis is placed on the constant collection and filtering of ideas, data, causes of discrepancies, potential solution strategies, and criteria that the organization would attend to as it moves forward. These have been summarized in various dated forms and tables. There is a chronology of information that should prove invaluable for prioritizing.

This record of the needs assessment is broad initially and comes to a narrower point with the passage of time. This visual image cannot be reinforced strongly enough. What has happened is that many needs have been distilled into carefully selected ones. Throughout the meetings of the NAC, the facilitator periodically reminds (updates) the group of the focusing process and uses en-route indicators to show progress.

❖ HOW TO APPROACH DATA ANALYSIS AND PRIORITIZATION

Before getting into details of the two activities facing the NAC, let's start with assumptions critical to understanding how to use this text. They are:

1. The focus is on data collected from activities done in Phase II of needs assessment. Valuable data have been obtained in Phase I and will be incorporated into analysis and prioritization.

2. There are simply too many methods to (or attempt to) provide analysis strategies for all of them. It would bog things down too much and would not be very utilitarian. Therefore decisions have been made to only include what is frequently used in needs assessment.

3. Qualitative methods while different from each other have enough similarity in terms of analysis to be treated as a generic topic. At the same time, be aware of their subtle differences as described throughout the KIT.

4. The nuts and bolts of analysis are the essence of the coverage rather than the minute details of how to treat data. The chapters will be fairly short and to the point with sufficient specification to help one get meaning from data.

5. Topics such as causal analysis and epidemiology are covered but not in depth.

So how do we approach these two important topics, data analysis and prioritization (see Figure 1.3)? First, our generic attack on qualitative data from group techniques or interviews is based on the themes that emerge from them as guidance for the decision-making process. Second, for quantitative data, we assume a good portion of it comes from surveys. Third, the next step will be to integrate the data from different sources into a meaningful whole that allows the NAC and others to move to the selection of the highest priorities. Inherent here is the idea to portray what has been learned in a focused way so that the main issues are clear. That portrayal contains information from Phase I and anything else that is pertinent (ideas about potential causes of needs, possible criteria for prioritizing, resources to resolve the problems once identified, barriers and facilitators of change, etc.). The task then proceeds into the determination of the most critical needs (discrepancies) for further consideration.

At the end of these activities is a prioritized list of needs and preliminary set of action steps for the organization to think about and deliberate. The NAC should always refer back to the concept of narrowing in on a smaller subset of concerns. Analysis and prioritization represent a culmination in needs assessment, and as such remember to *date* all tables of what has transpired and how final priorities were generated.

Figure 1.3   Generic Approach to Analysis and Priority Setting

Step 1 Analyze Qualitative Phase II Data in Term of Themes (Chapter 2)

Step 2 Analyze Quantitative Phase II Data in Terms of Discrepancies (Chapter 3)

Step 3 Integrate Data From Steps 1 and 2 Including Information From Phase I (Chapter 4)

Step 4 Determine Needs-Based Priorities (Chapter 5)

Step 5 Capitalize on Needs Assessment Work—A Challenge to Needs Assessors (Chapter 6)

Highlights of the Chapter

1. Needs, especially for major organizations, almost always arise from data collected from multiple constituencies by the use of multiple methods.

2. Multiple methods while strongly encouraged come with attendant problems for analysis.

3. The terms *within-method* and *between-method* variations were noted.

4. The nature of what is entailed in prioritizing needs was explained.

5. Assumptions underlying analysis and prioritization were offered.

6. Emphasis was placed on linking the above two processes to decision making.

7. The funnel aspect of the process was mentioned, and in relation to it the importance of good record keeping was underscored.

8. Finally, while the book deals with data collected in Phase II, information from Phase I is important for arriving at needs-based priorities.

2

Dealing With
Qualitative Needs Data

❖ INTRODUCTION

In this chapter we provide a general process for analyzing qualitative data. From one point of view, such data may not seem to be particularly relevant for analysis. It does not result in the measurement of discrepancies, which is at the core of the definition of need. In most circumstances, discrepancies have to be inferred from qualitative methods (observations, interviews, community forums, group discussions, and records containing narratives and comments) and therefore are suspect as to whether they are really indicators of needs. There may only be an implied sense of "what should be" as filtered through the interpretation of a facilitator and the needs assessment committee (NAC).

So why put emphasis on qualitative methods? There are numerous reasons making a strong case for their inclusion in needs assessment. First, it is neither wise nor sensible to accept the premise that quantitative data by themselves (ever) drive needs-based decisions. Certainly numbers help, but other factors enter in such as values, perceptions, the influence of others, historical understandings, and our backgrounds and willingness to commit time, energy, and resources to resolving problems underlying needs. Qualitative methods produce data that are invaluable in terms of values, how an entity is viewed, interest in getting behind a new endeavor, and so forth.

In many cases, they afford insights that are simply not there in the numbers. That is why we so often see congressional hearings that amplify other more quantitative testimony with a human face. What is found through qualitative methods may better reveal driving and compelling forces than what is learned from quantitative ones. The two methodologies in conjunction with each other offer a much stronger basis for needs assessment. In this regard, Example 2.1 underscores the importance of the concept of commitment.

Example 2.1

Commitment to a Manned Mission to Mars

In an address to the research forum of the Ohio Science and Engineering Alliance, the presenter (L. Reid, 2005, former head of engineers at the NASA Lewis facility) responded to an interesting question about the ability of NASA (the National Aeronautics and Space Administration) to mount a manned mission to Mars. The question was "Is it meaningful for us to think about a mission to Mars when it would take considerably more than 3 years to get there and the same amount of time for the return trip? How could we support and maintain people for that long in space?"

The reply was pondered and rather slow in coming back. It went something like this. "There are two parts to a response. If your question is about the know-how for accomplishing this mission, we've had that for a long time. Of course we have the technology, and it could be done. [Let this stand for the quantitative component of our work in needs assessment.] But the second part of the response is more complicated and is quite different from what we know about hardware and technology.

"It relates to whether we as a society have the will to commit to the task of developing the necessary machinery and to conducting the trip. Will we see it as a viable need and concern for our society? Would we be willing to devote the resources of human spirit, time, money, and so forth to do it? Will we see it as something that we as a nation should do? [In our analogy let this stand for the qualitative part of our process.]."

Quantitative methods generally cannot get at feelings and commitment, even when they contain a qualitative component (open-ended questions in a survey). Each method by itself leads to an incomplete picture of needs or phrased alternatively would not lead to a comprehensive understanding of them. Thus qualitative methods are essential for the needs process.

❖ FEATURES OF QUALITATIVE DATA THAT GUIDE ANALYSIS

Structured qualitative methods have been used in much of needs assessment. What is meant by "structured"? In most situations such methods are not used without some review of the literature and initial exploration of the situation and the nature of the problem. (See Book 3 in the KIT.) A lot of useful and critical thinking about the process has gone on before new data (qualitative and quantitative) are ever collected in Phase II.

When interviews, observations, focus groups, and so forth are employed, they invariably have a set of questions toward which they are directed. This is the structure. But at the same time, it is a flexible rather than rigid frame for data collection. It allows for open probing and attending to things that enhance the direction of the endeavor.

The questions have been presorted so that they represent the key features that we would like to learn about and are relevant to the needs decisions that will be made. They are tied into how we organize and treat data from qualitative sources. Although unexpected information might be obtained, the first attack on the data will be via the prespecified questions. This would apply to most qualitative methods in needs assessment. Tables and data analysis follow this pattern, and it simplifies the work.

❖ STRUCTURING IN DATA ANALYSIS

Table 2.1 contains an overview of main steps in handling qualitative data. The rationale behind them is also given. Before going into details of the table, one other activity is important to note:

Transcribe or collate all open-ended data (comments about needs made in writing, responses or issues raised in interviews) per question, making sure that those of individuals are kept separate. This is a format for easy skimming. (Many qualitative techniques do not use large samples so that the data can be quickly skimmed. Even when the data set is large, doing this is encouraged as noted in Table 2.1).

Table 2.1   Overview of the Qualitative Analysis Process

Procedural Aspect	Purpose/Description
Review the General Structure for the Qualitative Method Being Employed	Provides a guideline for the facilitator and needs assessment committee when starting the analysis process Keep in mind that structure is not a constraint but a game plan that is able to shift and adopt as the analysis progresses
Skim a Sample of the Qualitative Data	It is a good general rule to first scan whatever data have been collected to get a feel for their texture and nuances
Begin Analysis and Pull Out Variables	Go through the data (via computer or visual means) and list variables that seem to characterize the data Give these variables preliminary labels/names
Identifying Initial Data Categories (IDCs) per Question	Using what you generated from the above pull out the main variables (IDCs) that are emerging from open-ended data Reduces the information into a more meaningful form Helps get a more focused sense of what the data are telling us
Identifying Themes per Question	A higher level of data analysis that begins to get at meaning and unifying explanations underlying the IDCs Looking at the variables by structured question to see if a single higher-level construct or multiple constructs seem to fit (may be difficult especially when first thinking about this type of data)
Identifying Linking or Overarching Themes Across Questions	A higher level of analysis and probably the most meaningful Seeing connections across questions and thinking about a higher level of meaning May point toward areas where more information is needed

Procedural Aspect	Purpose/Description
Reviewing the Overarching Themes	How useful are these themes in terms of helping us view/understand needs?
	To what extent do they fit with the decision-oriented thinking of the organization?
	To what extent do they fit with other data about needs and at the same time what unique information do they afford?
Verify/Confirm the Quality of the Data	To what extent are independent analyses of the data similar and seeing the same things in the results?
	If similar, the credibility of results is enhanced

1. Look at the responses to get a feel for what they are saying (do not try to initially analyze them). Based on this preliminary scan are there patterns, recurring concepts, or threads running across questions? Do respondents seem to be using common terms or references when answering? Do this as a rough screening and as a limited form of immersion in the raw data.

   Perform an initial analysis of the data while keeping the area of the needs assessment in mind. There are two basic approaches with both relying on creating data categories of similar responses using the constant-comparative method. As you are doing either of them observe if there any quotes in the raw data that really capture or are a good illustration of a category. (Guard against fragmenting responses so that meaning becomes lost. You are looking for a response that is the essence of a category or variable.) The two approaches are:

   - Create by hand initial data categories (IDCs) by looking at each response and giving it or part of it a data label or in essence what is a variable name. Then go to the next response and repeat the procedure. Does the next response fit the prior IDC, or is it different? When data categories repeat, keep tallies.

   - Enter the data into a qualitative analysis program or use a database system that will facilitate an analysis very much like what was just described.

2. Perform a more in-depth data analysis. This step requires more sophisticated thinking about and probing of the data and is best accomplished if there has been a solid foundation established in Phase I of needs assessment including some reading of related literature. It is based on answering a number of questions of the data and IDCs that have been extracted from it.

- Are there themes that run through the answers? A theme is a unifying concept that connects all or some categories for a question.

- Are there themes that connect the responses and IDCs across questions? Are there concepts in the data that can be linked together? These have been labeled as overarching or explanatory themes (Altschuld, Kumar, Smith, & Goodway, 1999; Kumar & Altschuld, 1999).

- Are there questions coming from the analysis that require more data collection—albeit even a small amount of same?

- Are there categories that are missing or don't come up to any great degree? If important, would it be wise to do some additional exploration of them?

- Are the themes providing information that explains how the need is being perceived, and do they offer valuable input into the overall needs process?

- In doing this last step there will be a tendency to move from word descriptions of variables to more explanatory phrases or terminology (see Figure 2.1).

3. Seek an external peer review (one or more individuals) of what has been generated from the above steps with an emphasis on the IDCs, themes per question, and themes across questions.

- Since analysis is tedious and labor intensive, involving others for confirmatory purposes should be done with a small, random subset of the data.

- If more than one person has been involved in data collection, have each person conduct an independent analysis and see the degree to which the two analyses are similar or different.

- Ask the external peers about the flow of logic of the analysis and whether or not it is sensible. If they do not feel it is, more data coming from interviews, another focus group interview, or the use of another qualitative method might be desirable.

Figure 2.1   Schematic Going From Raw Open-Ended Data to Overarching Explanatory Themes

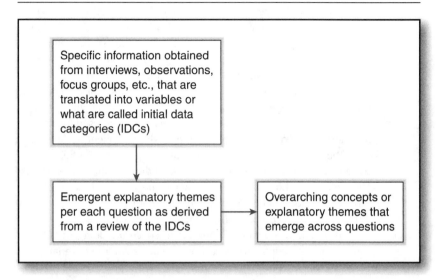

The picture depicted in Figure 2.1 is worth a thousand words. It is derived from a qualitative evaluation (Kumar & Altschuld, 1999) and illustrates moving from IDCs to overarching, emerging, and linking themes. It provides a sense of going from specific to more expansive understandings (in the context of individual questions and across questions) and is a model for many of the principles just espoused for analyzing qualitative data (see Example 2.2).

Example 2.2

Working With Complex Qualitative Data

How were the data depicted in Figure 2.1 collected and analyzed? Kumar and Altschuld (1999) were looking at the implementation and impact of a novel teacher training program that was heavily invested in technology for its delivery. Their investigation consisted of in-depth individual interviews with students, faculty, and administrators and observations made on campus and in local schools. During the interviews the evaluators noticed that students felt that they might not be able to apply certain aspects of their training when they began teaching.

From that concern and knowing that the data obtained at the university were insufficient on the point, the authors returned to the site several months

(Continued)

(Continued)

later and went to schools where graduates were teaching. They added questions to the interview about the longer-term utility of the training and what might facilitate and/or prevent its use in the reality of public school settings. By this means factors were uncovered that university staff were unaware of and that were affecting their students who were in teaching careers.

One idea that comes out of this is that successive waves of qualitative methods can be quite beneficial for gaining subtle, in-depth understanding of intricate situations. In this case, the initial interviews were used to shape later ones and allowed for the generation and subsequent testing of hypotheses. The investigators gained perspective by going to the field and observing teachers in their natural habitat. Indeed they felt that the experience enhanced their ability to critically attack the data and to develop themes, especially those that were overarching in nature.

The interviews were audiotaped, and notes were made as they were underway on forms that contained appropriate space for doing so. One team member had transcripts produced from the tapes and did his analysis from them. The other only used notes without the transcripts. Thus there was a way to independently verify findings. The researchers, who were from different states, were in contact but not in regard to the analysis.

The initial data categories they produced were a synthesis across the variables they identified. Sometimes the terms or labels in the individual analyses were a bit different, but the overall agreement was above 80% and it was a relatively easy process to arrive at final labels and a consensus list of variables. Producing themes for questions and overarching themes was nowhere near as easy.

One of the investigators had much more experience with this type of data than the other and had used the methodology in a number of other studies. That background was helpful in generating a beginning set of themes and providing a brief description of what they were about and how they related to the main area of concern. The second author, due to less exposure to the technique, had a more difficult time arriving at themes.

The two investigators independently doing the analysis had another benefit. The overarching themes were presented by one to the other not as a *fait accompli* but as a possible model of factors that might help in seeing what was happening. The second person then reacted to them in terms of whether they were realistic, whether they truly seemed linked to the data and variables, whether they offered insights into the use or lack thereof of the innovation, whether they would be defensible to others, and other similar concerns. The final categories were an outcome of that discussion.

With a resource like a needs assessment committee it is quite possible to utilize procedures like these for qualitative data. The atmosphere for posing themes must be an open one where they are fair game for challenge and debate. If such conditions are not established, bias can and certainly will occur.

Similar logic and thinking can be applied to needs assessment. It is important to note that the external evaluators in the example had access to data from an internal quantitative study. Those results in concert with the qualitative ones led to a comprehensive view of what the innovative program was doing. The combination of the two approaches made each more salient.

Please note in Figure 2.1 that some IDCs by themselves may not weigh heavily in the determination of emergent themes. The latter were more valuable and impressive to university staff and helped show what was happening as a result of the training.

Several other lessons come from the example. Questions regarding type of qualitative data collection involve whether there is an adequate sample size, what groups should be included, how they should be sampled, replication, and how the results should be reported. In Table 2.2 each question is addressed along with how it might be handled.

Table 2.2 Analysis-Related Questions for Qualitative Needs Assessment Data

Question	Commentary
What is an adequate sample size for qualitative data?	There is no single answer to the question inasmuch as some techniques require large numbers (community group forums) and others are for small groups (the nominal group technique).
	One good rule is to not seek more sample if no new data seem to be emerging; the cost is not worth it. In many cases after 6–8 individual interviews not much in the way of additional information is being collected. Do a few more interviews, perhaps for credibility (faith in larger numbers) rather than for any other reason.
	Judge what sample size might satisfy or seem to fit the decision-making context. What would be seen as acceptable to the decision makers?
Who should be included in the sample? (What groups?)	A simple reply would be representatives of all involved or stakeholding groups.
	In needs assessment there are three levels of involvement. So if possible and important to the assessment include individuals from each of them.
	Treat each level separately for analysis before comparing and collapsing results.
	One thing to remember is that most often needs assessments are done at Level 1 (service recipients) and Level 2 (service deliverers). Level 3 (the overall system) assessments are sometimes done after the data from 1 and 2 have been analyzed and interpreted.

(Continued)

Table 2.2 (Continued)

Question	Commentary
How should the group(s) be sampled (what mechanisms should be used for obtaining the sample)?	If a purpose of the analysis is to generalize widely, you might want to employ random sampling even with qualitative methods provided that criteria for inclusion of individuals have been met. Most often, involvement in qualitative methods is based not on random but on purposive sampling. - Are important groups fully represented in the community forum? - Has the right balance of key community informants been sampled?
What about the notion of replication?	Replication is the name of the game. Confidence in results is always enhanced by replication of focus groups, interviews, observations, and the like. As with sample size, replication adds expense, time, and wear on the needs assessment committee and others involved in the endeavor. It is recommended that funds be set aside to accommodate some replication or collection of corroborative data, if required.
How do the above questions affect the reporting of results, and what effect might they have on needs-based decision making?	All of the questions and what is entailed in answering them have a very large impact on analysis and reporting. Here are a few illustrations: - Involving more than one of the three levels may make the development of instruments more difficult and in turn will have an effect on reports that are written. - As the process of assessment becomes complicated the amount of time and effort required to process and integrate data will be larger than for a simpler one. - Results have to be summarized and placed in a format that assists decision makers as they come to agreement on directions for the organization and the commitment of resources (this may not be particularly easy when there are many parts of the process). - Overall the process and generation of final reports and recommendations will be elongated.

❖ SO YOU HAVE ANALYZED THE DATA—NOW WHAT?

From the question above, it is obvious that the analysis has to be followed by considerations of how to present qualitative results both as a stand alone product and with those obtained from quantitative methods. Certainly procedures have to be described so that decision makers have faith in how the data were collected and for predicating their choices on the quality of what was implemented. Be sure to include *short* sections that explain the purpose of the information that was collected, sampling, the nature of the methodology, the general strategy of analysis, how the validity of the data (external analysis or parallel analyses) was determined, and any problems encountered during the undertaking. If there are caveats in determining needs-based policy or action-oriented options, clearly indicate them.

The word *short* is underlined. The intent of the report is not to be a methodological treatise but to be one that sees methodology as a pathway to the main findings and what they mean for the assessment. For that reason place a lot of the details in appendices and don't crowd them into the body of the report. If you do, attention will be needlessly diverted. Some appendices contain transcripts or other raw forms of the data, expanded discussions of samples involved in focus groups or individual interviews, how observations were conducted, and so forth.

The focus of the report is to inform decision making. After brief descriptions, the IDCs (per group/source) should be portrayed followed by tables containing the general or overarching themes that have been derived from each source/group. These are the key ingredients.

What would be ideal from this base is a summary table showing the themes that were in consensus across groups and sources and those that were in agreement for several sources and for which there was no conflicting evidence or perceptions. It is also wise to point out that there may be issues for which agreement has not been achieved, bones of contention, and factoids that stand apart and may represent troublesome considerations. These could be important for decision making and noted in the report that is generated.

Throughout the KIT stress has been placed on *dating* all tables. Doing so is valuable for documenting the process and for tracking how the NAC and needs assessor arrived at their conclusions. It also allows the committee, if necessary, to back away from summarized data and return to original responses.

Lastly, go back to a part of the summary process that was glossed over but will arise later in dealing with data analysis and reporting. Needs assessment almost always consists of mixing quantitative and qualitative methods. That means the qualitative analysis and reporting is a piece of a much larger and intricate portrait. What must be done is to weave the qualitative methods into the more subtle and difficult tapestry of the overall investigation. Such a perspective will be introduced later in this text.

Highlights of the Chapter

1. The value and necessity of qualitative methods was itself a theme throughout this chapter.

2. An overview of generic steps that could be used to analyze most qualitative data was provided.

3. The steps were based on the idea that nearly all qualitative procedures have been heavily prestructured and that is useful for creating meaning from the data.

4. A number of questions about qualitative methods were posed as a backdrop for thinking about how to report findings.

5. The concept in the final report for qualitative methods is to place most of the details of methods into appendices and only include summaries in the text.

6. The bulk of the report should concentrate on overarching, explanatory themes that appear to be consistently supported across data sources and groups.

7. Remember that at some point in analysis and reporting, the NAC and the facilitator will be integrating quantitative and qualitative results into a coherent, meaningful whole in regard to needs.

3

Coping With Quantitative Needs Data

❖ INTRODUCTION

Quantitative data are prominent in the needs assessment process. Numbers permit the calculation of a discrepancy, which is central to the "needs/gap" construct and important for prioritization and development of solution strategies. Nearly all investigations of need use quantitative procedures such as surveys, epidemiological studies, and database analyses. Because surveys are so common in this context (Mosely & Heaney, 1994), they will be the main focus of this chapter. Before getting into them let's briefly consider records and epidemiological sources.

Organizations such as health care providers, educational systems, government agencies, and businesses routinely collect and maintain information on many different variables (Guercio, 2001). A utilitarian example of a data repository is the Pacific Regional Education Library Needs Analysis and Response Unit. Its objective is to collect and disseminate needs-type information about demographics, school systems, educational outcomes and impacts, and health-related statistics. It does this through relational databases in the region (Braun, Hammond, & Kana'iaupuni, 2006).

Passmore (1990) noted that archives provide data on an array of consumer variables such as health perceptions and related concerns (smoking, obesity) and occupational safety. In the area of training needs assessment he demonstrated how a large data set of coal miner records (78,741) with work-related injuries (8,567) could be used to identify frequent and consequential training problems. At the same time, he noted that potential solution strategies were often difficult to observe from epidemiological analyses. Going to that level requires subtle inferences and other information before translation into policy and action.

Guidance on the analysis of a variety of types of quantitative needs data was presented by Altschuld and Witkin (2000). Their work is extended here with the stress as noted on various forms of surveys (mail, phone, or Web-based) in terms of "What do respondents tell us about needs, current and desired states, and deficiencies (gaps)?" The answer partly resides on how much confidence the needs assessment committee (NAC) puts in the quantitative results.

❖ SURVEY DATA ANALYSIS

First, we must look at the quality of the data themselves. Passing over this step too quickly can have serious implications for the needs assessment. From there, how are data queried for answers to needs questions, what certainty can be ascribed to them, and what might be ways to present the results to various audiences?

Spreadsheets and other software are useful in handling and analyzing quantitative data. While statistical computer programs may require additional resources and specialized training, it is not necessary that everyone involved in the process have this type of expertise. Working with spreadsheets is fairly common, and data can be easily imported into programs like SPSS and SAS for later analyses. In Table 3.1 are examples of real-world needs assessment survey work. In general, the five studies distributed surveys to multiple populations (clients, providers, etc.), offering a mechanism for triangulating findings and understanding them from the viewpoint of varied stakeholders. This allows the NAC and its facilitator to see agreements and disagreements between participating groups.

Table 3.1   Characteristics of Sources

Description	Location	Sample Size	Data Collection Method	Population(s)
Applied Survey Research, 1999, 2002	Santa Ana, CA	604	Interviews	Orange County homeless population
Chatelle & Tornquist, 2007	Texas	1,114 clients, 141 providers/ 752 contributors	Surveys	Clients, providers, and community
Satcher, Kosecoff, & Fink, 1980	Los Angeles (Watts area)	724 consumers, 224 providers, and 74 administrators	Staff- and self-administered surveys	Consumers, providers, and community
Chauvin, Anderson, & Bowdish, 2001	Southeastern United States	838	Surveys	Public health preparedness project
Lee, Altschuld, & White, 2007a	Ohio	145 students and 86 faculty and administrators	Electronic surveys	Minority college students

❖   PREANALYSIS DATA CHECKS

Begin by checking the information since errors can affect the validity and interpretation of numbers. Surveys may be delivered manually or electronically, but regardless of how they are administered, errors occur. All data must be translated or coded before analysis. Three methods of doing this are hand entry or keying from printed forms, scanning, and exporting/importing data from Web-based platforms such as Zoomerang, SurveyMonkey, or other providers.

Hand entering survey data is the most laborious and error-prone method. When possible, it should be avoided. Realistically, however, there are situations that may not afford any other approach. Small townships or community groups with limited resources might rely on volunteers with little guidance or training on how to enter data into a spreadsheet. Errors take place when individuals become distracted or fatigued and make keystroke mistakes (also referred to as mis-keying). They may skip an entry or input an incorrect code, which results in all of the subsequent entries in the spreadsheet being in the wrong cell or cells. This creates a distorted distribution of results due to the data in a row or a column being misaligned. This is referred to as truncation, and it throws off all the data after that particular row or column in the data set. For example, if the last row of data is missing a large number of entries, it may be a mistake to assume the survey ended with the preceding question or that there were a lot of nonresponses taking place at that point on the survey. A straightforward solution to this problem is to use two people with one calling out responses and the other entering the information. Despite this precaution, random checks are necessary to ensure the integrity of the data.

Optical scanning utilizes specialized forms for surveys. Respondents typically complete the scaled form, using a #2 lead pencil, which is entered into a computer via scanning hardware or software (available from vendors such as Scantron). Errors that occur with these forms are incorrect marking such as making more than one choice and erasures. Another dilemma is the failure of some scanning software and hardware to register responses when the respondent uses an ink pen. Problems like these should be identified and corrected by checks on the quality of the data. Questionable surveys should be reviewed for re-inputting or rescanning as well as having decision rules specifying when they should be omitted. The facilitator and/or NAC members should visually examine completed forms prior to statistical procedures in regard to their status.

Electronic surveys are increasingly popular (Anderson & Kanuka, 2003; Archer 2003; Shannon, Johnson, Searcy, & Lott, 2002; Stanton & Rogelberg, 2001) and have changed the process (Gunn, 2002). This popularity has resulted in some Internet-based surveys being quite inexpensive (as low as $20 per month). These instruments possess advantages over the traditional pencil-and-paper approach. Their interactive capabilities permit the use of video and audio directions to the respondents for faster completion. The systems have the capacity to study how much time respondents spend on selecting different items. The feature of greatest importance for analysis is the capacity to export the data into statistical software programs. This eliminates problems associated with hand processing.

Online surveys do have disadvantages. Response rates tend to be much lower (Dillman, 2000, 2004), and therefore larger sampling frames are required. The surveys do not work well with groups unfamiliar with computers, low-income households, the visually (or physically) impaired (as the authors are encountering in a current project), some immigrant groups, or those without access to or phobic about computers. Because of the visual aspects of electronic media, attention must be given to appearance when constructing instruments. Be attentive to the limitations of spacing, formatting, and the use of multiple scales before opting for an online survey.

In addition programming errors may arise during the data importing and exporting routines when using the services of a commercial provider. The point is that no matter the approach (electronic or otherwise) there should always be data checks. This is especially important if there are multiple data collection points. Do the data appear to be missing at random, or is there a pattern with specific questions left unanswered? Be attentive to anomalies in the scoring of variables such as responses outside of the scale range. This can come from either miscoding or the row or columns becoming misaligned (truncated), each of which creates difficulties in analysis. Due to the proliferation of online surveys concerns about data quality have been noted by a number of authors (DiLalla & Dollinger, 2006; Tabachnik & Fidell, 2006). Here are a few suggestions from Wulder (2008):

1. Inspect single variables for accurate input.

2. Check for missing data and determine why.

3. Identify and deal with outlier responses.

4. Evaluate the data to see if they appear to behave in unexpected ways such as unusual spread of responses within groups.

5. Evaluate the data to see if some variables seem to correlate more than anticipated, thus indicating they are measuring the same concept.

DiLalla and Dollinger (2006) recommended handling missing data by screening for invalid or out-of-range responses. One way to do this is via a matrix with the rows representing each respondent and the columns variables. Reading from left to right the responses for each individual can quickly be looked at by the facilitator and/or NAC members. Table 3.2 contains the responses given to two "needs" and two "background" items (gender and age). Based on a 6-point scale, several things are apparent. First Subject 3 did not respond to two items in the survey. This happens frequently in the assessment of needs and is more noticeable when double or triple scales are used. Second, the responses from Subject 5 depict how truncated data might appear.

Table 3.2 Sample Data Matrix

| | Needs Assessment Items | | | | Demographic | |
| | Need Item_1 | | Need Item_2 | | | |
	Current ("What Is") Condition	Desired ("What Should Be") Condition	Current ("What Is") Condition	Desired ("What Should Be") Condition	Gender	Age
Subject_1	3	5	6	4	1	45
Subject_2	4	6	5	5	2	38
Subject_3	4	6	4	M	1	M
Subject_4	3	5	6	M	2	50
Subject_5	M	3	5	4	4	1
Subject_n	4	M	5	M	M	38

M = missing data

The "should be" response in Item 1 is suspiciously low, and unless a 1-year-old child completed the survey, all of the data inputs may have been shifted to the right by one column. It is likely that Subject 5 opted not to respond to the age question. Another point to consider is the subtle information that is embedded in the descriptive results. As an illustration, responses that show large spreads for current status (in contrast to desired state) could indicate a lack of knowledge by many in the sample.

The raw data should be inspected especially if respondents have raised concerns about the survey in open-ended comments. Always undertake a thorough examination for errors such as misalignment (truncation) or misinterpretation of scales and watch for missing responses. Working across the rows, "holes" in the data could indicate someone either forgot or chose not to respond to a question. Looking down the columns, a high number of missing responses might relate to the suitability of the variable for the survey. There are other reasons for missing data. Surveys can be complex, hard to navigate, and time consuming. Nonresponse rates tend to increase with multiple scales (observed by Hamann in 1997 and partially seen by Lee, Altschuld, & White, 2007b) even for sophisticated respondents. The instructions may have to be reread for pencil-and-paper instruments or on how to navigate a Web-based survey particularly when drop-down menus are used. They can make the instrument difficult to complete.

It is not uncommon to have missing data with demanding surveys. They may appear challenging, or another possibility is that respondents may have opinions about a topic not in the list of options. One way to address such issues is to use proxy measures. After finding that health care consumers in the Los Angeles area had difficulty rating "feasibility," Satcher, Kosecoff, and Fink (1980) used "importance" as a substitute for "what should be" and "availability" for "what is" conditions.

Statistical software permits the identification of individuals or variables for deletion from the analysis. An excessive amount of missing data can be deleted at the respondent and variable levels. One easy tactic is to analyze only the needs assessment data with complete responses to all items. This practice may lead to some or considerable bias in results due to the smaller subset of respondents analyzed. Results can be quite problematic with small groups and lots of missing data. If the deletion approach is applied there may be less confidence in the results.

Some needs assessors impute means for dealing with missing data. These procedures rely on filling in the missing values by substitution or estimating replacement values. Several technical and somewhat statistically complicated methods are available such as the use of historical records or a pool of donors with similar characteristics to the group of interest (Chambers, 2005). Whatever the method, caution must be exercised when it comes to interpretation as the data did not come directly from the sample. In an investigation of needs in programs designed to improve the retention rates for minority students in science, technology, engineering, and mathematics (STEM), Lee et al. (2007b) posited that imputation causes other subtle problems in data analysis and opted not to use it in their study. What to do may be dependent on the specific context, and the reader is referred to the reference for the rationale for not imputing.

Further into the analysis process, the last step is to calculate discrepancy values by subtracting the actual or "current condition" responses from the "desired condition" ones. If multiple scales are used, the assessor next calculates averages for the other scales associated with the need. What are the respondents' level of motivation to address the discrepancy and perceptions about the feasibility of possible solution strategies? Mean scores, standard deviations, and/or related statistics are usually generated for individual items and the overall scales from which they come. Averaging across items is justified because they are perceived to collectively represent an entire concept (DeVellis, 2003).

❖ DATA ANALYSIS QUESTIONS

Needs assessment surveys may be used once or periodically (say every 3 to 5 years). In the latter comparisons over time can be made such as in a statewide assessment of school nutrition (Bunch, 1980; Bunch & Watson, 1986; Watson & Bunch, 1983). In either case, once data quality checks have been done, the NAC or analyst proceeds with a sense of trustworthiness and legitimacy in probing deeply into what the survey respondents are saying. Questions here are:

1. Who are the respondents?

2. Who participated in the survey, interviews, or other sources of information, and are subclusters of individuals evident in the data set?

3. What are their characteristics (demographic, socioeconomic, etc.), and did we get the respondents anticipated when originally planning the assessment?

4. Is the sample large enough for analysis, and did we get adequate representation (size, proportionality)?

5. Do any unexpected subgroups pop up in the sample?

6. Do the subgroups have different perspectives and opinions about items or issues?

7. Were there key groups of stakeholders that did not respond? What might this say about the conclusions drawn and implications for developing solutions to resolve needs?

The bottom line is whom do the respondents represent?

The next step is summarizing the needs assessment data in descriptive statistics as suggested above (mean, variances, standard deviation). Frequencies and proportions portray responses in ways that are understood and accepted by most decision-making audiences. A simple rule is that the data should be presented in a clear and coherent fashion. This is thought about early in the investigation but may be refined after data are collected.

Another feature of summarizing data may entail comparing values obtained to another group or known population. In epidemiological studies, this refers to how well the characteristics of the sample match those of the population of interest. The better the fit, the greater the opportunity to generalize the results. From there we could proceed to finer subgroup analysis in accord with the demographic characteristics of the respondents. In Table 3.3 are some ideas on possible combinations and the selected statistics for any needs assessment.

Table 3.3   Questions in Quantitative Analysis of Needs Assessment Survey Data

Question	Variables	Statistics
How can we check the data prior to analysis?	Use the data quality matrix	(1) Counts and patterns of missing data, (2) out-of-range values, and (3) number of "not applicable" responses
How can we describe the sample data?	Age, gender, socioeconomic status, race/ ethnicity, income, occupation, education, organizational status, expertise, etc.	Frequency counts, proportions, percentages, averages (mean, median, mode), variances (standard deviation), etc.
How can we describe the psychometric quality of the measured responses?	Multiple items focused on a need, a theme, a concept, or some other dimension	Reliability, validity measures of overall scales and/or the subscales within them Intercorrelations of scales and/or variables
How can we describe the variables of interest?	Each individual variable and associated discrepancies	Frequency counts, measures of central tendency (means) and dispersion (range, variances, etc.)
How can we describe the relationship among variables?	Paired sets of variables	Correlation and regression analysis, means difference analysis, weighted needs analysis, proportional reduction in error (see Book 1 in the KIT for a number of these procedures)
How can we evaluate the overall statistical conclusion of the results?	Across all the statistical tests undertaken in the needs assessment	Power, statistical significance (p-values), effect size (how large of a discrepancy) See quality ideas at the end of the chapter

The traditional distinction between descriptive and inferential statistics is that the former yields summaries of the data and the latter helps in probing into subtle dimensions important to an assessment. Inferential procedures are used to test statistical differences between groups or subgroups in the study on one or more key variables. While describing the participants in a training needs assessment, it is important and vital to know if they hold varied perceptions of training needs based on the position they hold in the organization's hierarchy. By using inferential statistics we can determine whether such differences are real rather than due to random error or chance.

Descriptive-type comparisons are found in Lee, Altschuld, and White (2007a, 2007b). They examined the differences on survey questions between minority students and university faculty/administrators. They asked the two groups to "explain" on a subsequent open-ended survey why they differed on certain aspects of need. Items not in agreement were displayed in graphs for those receiving the subsequent survey. This approach yielded sharply disparate patterns of thinking, which were simply provided in tables. Formal tests could have been conducted, but the descriptive approach was the most utilitarian way to make the point. The concept is to seek the most direct mechanism for displaying data.

Interestingly, in their study they collected information from first-year to fourth-year students but did not compare these groups. Most assessments include quite a few demographic indicators, so many potential contrasts could be made. The NAC will always have to think about which comparisons to make (driven by either the literature or the situation).

❖ RESPONDENT CHARACTERISTICS

Obviously it is valuable to deal with the nature of those responding to the data collection effort. A sample can be thought of by variables such as age, gender, race/ethnicity, education, occupation, and socioeconomic status. Needs generally have to be disaggregated and are specific in terms of subgroups. An example from a community-based needs assessment illustrates this point (Chatelle & Tornquist, 2007).

Compiled for the Greater Longview United Way in Texas, survey data were collected from three groups: 1,114 social service clients (Level 1), 141 social service providers (Level 2), and 752 community members (subset of Level 3) who supported funding through the local agency. This reflects good practice by focusing on the three levels with the first two having more direct contact with and sensitivity to needs than the more distant community respondents.

The team conducting this effort described the characteristics of the Level 1 sample in regard to age, race/ethnicity, household size, annual income, length of residency, and employment status. These variables allowed the needs assessors to "drill down" into the data to determine if there were unique aspects within subgroup responses. In the initial design of a survey consider how demographic variables might be used to explore the area of concern.

To illustrate a subgroup analysis, consider a training needs assessment conducted for the National Institute of Corrections (Clem, 2003). From four levels of correction management (executives, senior managers, operational managers, and supervisors) the NAC was able to make distinctions based on the extent of interaction with the inmate population. More contact with the service population (prisoners) was detected across the lower levels of the hierarchy, and for the higher levels it was more abstract.

Groups can see things similarly, or they may have considerably disparate views. Were the training needs differentiated for the four groups, and were trends apparent? It is also possible to read other needs into the data such as communication gaps that lead to barriers in training (receptivity, participation, etc.) unless addressed. Managers might see training as important and even fund it while staff may not value it or desire that it be on another topic. If such things are not thought through, the results could be less effective training and negative effects on organizational morale. Seemingly straightforward survey data may not be that simple, and the data often point to more than meets the eye. Consider plausible alternative explanations of data.

It should be noted the concept applies equally to qualitative data from focus groups, interviews, and observations. In terms of observations, consider whether the appropriate cases were selected, how well they fit the focus of the needs assessment, whether they contain a sufficient range of events that should be addressed, and so forth. By representatively selecting and describing participants and the nature of the circumstances observed, we enhance the validity of the needs assessment and ultimately the trust placed in results. The NAC must think about what the findings would mean and how they would be valued within the organizational decision-making context. This is important as organizational resources, goals, and individuals will often be impacted by the process and outcomes of an assessment.

❖ DESCRIPTIVE STATISTICS

The rationale for computing descriptive statistics is to collapse the data into indices that depict the respondents' position on an item. Frequency distribution, mean scores, variances, and standard deviations are typically computed for each of the "what is" and "what should be" scales and items on the instrument. Frequency distributions are employed to see how the subjects allocated their ratings for each item and the point around which they congregate. Frequencies and the spread (dispersion) of responses are two concepts extremely useful for understanding and interpreting needs assessment data. For example, suppose you have a "what should be" scale in which there seems to be two center points (bimodal distribution) and a wide range of scores. It is apparent that the respondents split on the item (see Example 3.1). This is not uncommon and indicates that there were two unique positions on an issue or a topic or that there were distinct groups of respondents.

Example 3.1

What Can Happen With Apparently Simple Data!

A needs assessment format was used to evaluate the performance of the chair of a large academic department in a major university. Performance was divided into six cluster areas. Faculty and staff were asked to rate items on importance and the extent to which they were achieved by the chair. More than 70% of the intended sample completed the anonymous survey.

To the chagrin of one of the coauthors, in nearly all of the clusters, the response patterns were bimodal with one being negative on the chair's work and the other being positive. If only averages were looked at, the results would be somewhat below the midpoint. But after closer examination of the data it became apparent that the negative ratings were consistent, were extremely low, and came from considerably more than half the individuals who completed the evaluation. Open-ended comments were parallel to the ratings and were even more overwhelmingly negative. Moreover, major gaps (discrepancies) were notable in the data when total group averages for importance and achievement were examined. They were there in all six clusters, and almost two thirds of the items were demonstrating this pattern.

A few other points relevant to needs assessment are notable in the example. First, almost all respondents were in agreement about the importance of the items. The ratings were uniformly high with the achievement ratings being the main contributors to defining the discrepancies. When thinking about needs sometimes only one side of the equation (the "what is") seems to have much variability. Second, it was suggested after the data were summarized that it might have been better to ask the respondents to rank-order the 6 categories once they had completed their ratings. Were some more important than others? Lastly, politics quickly came to the fore with a few individuals in the department (including the chair) trying to kill the report (a constant theme is that assessments of need have a subtle but prominent "dark side").

Indeed the coauthor was threatened with repercussions if the report was made available to all involved stakeholders. Fortunately with backing from several key committee members it was, and it led to the chair not continuing in the position. Data collected in a public forum is public information.

Going deeper into double scaling, let's examine a Web-based survey conducted by a social service agency. Two groups, supervisors and supervisees, rated a set of task statements pertaining to productivity with case management software. The scales consisted of "current" and "desired" capability, with anchors from "novice" to "expert."

Assume 25 employees and 13 supervisors responded. After collapsing the groups ($n = 38$), a frequency distribution for a single task item might look like the one in Table 3.4. The frequency of the "present capability" shows a preponderance of ratings on the novice end of the 4-point scale with fewer individuals seeing themselves as experts. Thus present capability self-estimated as low and desired is high, indicative of training needs. Other possible patterns include high present and low desired states, or both distributions could be relatively equal (high or low).

Table 3.4   Frequencies for Double-Scaled Data

					Anchor Scales: 1 (Novice) to 4 (Expert)				
	Present Capability					Desired Capability			
Item #	1 f	2 f	3 f	4 f	Task	1 f	2 f	3 f	4 f
1	13	12	9	4	Uses work group calendar to schedule meetings and rooms	5	10	11	12

When the present condition is high and the desired is low, this rules out a need. Indeed, if any training is being provided, the organization should reconsider why it is doing so. If the pattern is high-high the skill will be deemed important, but there is no discrepancy and hence no need. If low-low, then the majority of respondents are suggesting that they do not desire training or see it as being important.

This example, although contrived, also suggests the need to disaggregate the data by respondent groups (employees and supervisors) and focus on resulting patterns in the data to create information. These situations are routine in assessment. They underscore why there is a desire to use a third scale in training situations such as motivation, feasibility, likelihood of participating in solutions, and so forth as another input into thinking about gaps and ways to resolve those that are observed. This could reduce response rates by making the survey more complicated to complete and time consuming, but the added value may be necessary and the loss of some returns is offset by the gain in information.

Central tendency is an important statistic for the current and desired state in regard to needs. Different estimates are used for different circumstances, but the arithmetic mean, median, and mode are most often reported. Other approaches are magnitude estimation scaling based on ratio scores (with the geometric mean as the central tendency) and the trimmed mean (Dell, 1974). The trimmed mean is calculated after discarding equal amounts of very high and very low scores. For the numeric scales usually employed in needs assessments, the mode and the median are the correct statistics to use. In practice frequent violations of this are seen, and means tend to be reported more than other measures of central tendency.

As in the bimodal example, we must be concerned with the variability around the measure of central tendency. Do the respondents cluster near the center, or are they more dispersed? For the mean, the standard deviation and variance are calculated. They allow us to see to what extent a specific score deviates from the mean. For the mode and median, the measures of variability are the range (highest minus lowest) and the interquartile range (IQR). By dividing a data set into four equal parts, three quartiles are created, which represent the 25th, 50th, and 75th percentiles (referred to as Q1, Q2, and Q3). The IQR is determined by subtracting the value of Q1 from that of Q3 (one could additionally employ the semi-interquartile range, SIQR). For an application of quartiles in a study of needs in education see Hung, Altschuld, and Lee (2008) or in health care see Williams, Harris, and Turner-Stokes (2007).

Individual items in a scale can be added together to create composites (multiple statements pertaining to a specific task or topic) organized or clustered in a conceptual way. Rather than a single item, the descriptive question shifts to the composite or overall score for a set of related items. Going back to the office training example, the measures of central tendency and variability can be computed for word process-ing skills that support the creation of reports required by funding sources and desktop publishing with its emphasis on communication with the organization's constituencies (see Table 3.5).

Table 3.5   Data Table for Clustered Items

Items	Delta Δ	Desired Capability* Novice (1) – Expert (4)	Task Cluster	Present Capability* Novice (1) – Expert (4)
1–4	0.10	3.15	Word processing	3.25
5–8	–0.70	3.35	Desktop publishing	2.65
9–12	–0.65	3.65	Spreadsheets	3.00
13–16	–1.10	3.98	Relational databases	2.88

*Numbers in columns 3 and 5 average (mean) scores

The word processing tasks are almost equal on the "present" and "desired" states, but the desktop publishing ones are lower on "present" than on "desired" capability. This suggests a preference for desk-top publishing training compared to word processing. By clustering similar items, patterns can be spotted. The discrepancies are indicated as "Delta" in the table. The analyst should be sensitive to the impor-tance of "not applicable" (NA) and "don't know" (DK) responses as information about items. A large number of such responses indicate that the sample is not knowledgeable enough to provide ratings or to answer the questions being asked.

As a rule and as fits the needs area of concern, consider having more than two scales per item (emphasized earlier). Setting aside the burden imposed on respondents and effects on response rates, what impact does this have on the results, the NA category (it could change the response rate or raise it by allowing respondents more categories by which to tell us where their understanding is), and other aspects of the survey? One use of three scales was by Satcher et al. (1980), who conducted a community-based assessment where 38 health services were rated on three scales: importance, feasibility,

and availability. Responses were provided by a sample of administrators, service providers, and patients. The assessment concentrated
on the first two levels, and the use of administrators provided a limited Level 3 perspective. Table 3.6 contains the scaling and rating levels
used in this study.

Table 3.6 Triple-Scaled Needs Assessment Survey

Item #	Importance	Need Area	Availability	Feasibility
Item_1	1 – 2 – 3 – 4 – 5	Statement_1	1 – 2 – 3	1 – 2 – 3
Item_2	1 – 2 – 3 – 4 – 5	Statement_2	1 – 2 – 3	1 – 2 – 3
Item_3	1 – 2 – 3 – 4 – 5	Statement_3	1 – 2 – 3	1 – 2 – 3
Item_4	1 – 2 – 3 – 4 – 5	Statement_4	1 – 2 – 3	1 – 2 – 3

Note: A 3-point scale was used for availability and feasibility.

Doing these types of things will challenge the NAC in how it han-
dles and interprets very complex yet valuable data. The formatting of
the three scales has been discussed in Book 1 of this KIT. Visually one
could place the stem on the left side of the page followed by the three
scales on the right side. This kind of surveying leads to a three-way
configuration of mean scores across dimensions that provide much
information for understanding needs.

There are rich possibilities in the data. If importance is viewed as
the most critical dimension, you could begin by disregarding items
with low importance means (bear in mind that some standard for
making this judgment is required—what constitutes low importance). Kosecoff and Fink (1982) prescribed courses of action for
importance with decisions resting on the "availability" and "feasibility" of providing medical services to clients (Table 3.7). The table
is an illustration of how cutoff decisions can be made by the NAC
and communicated to the organization. It is a strategy for bringing
others (community stakeholders) into the process and getting them
involved in the subtle nature of needs-based decision making.
Specific need statement numbers (with a legend) can be placed in the
table cells to show the distribution across the combinations of
dimensions. Table 3.7 is analogous to the quadrant method proposed
by Hershkowitz (1974).

Table 3.7   Summary of a Way to Think About Triple-Scaled Needs

	Availability Is High		*Availability Is Low*	
	High Feasibility	*Low Feasibility*	*High Feasibility*	*Low Feasibility*
High Importance	No action needed by the organization on these items (services)	What is cost to organization to provide these items (services)?	Organization should focus on these items (services)	Further study by organization required on these items (services)
Low Importance	Items (or services) rated here require no further action	Items (or services) rated here require no further action	Items (or services) rated here require no further action	Items (or services) rated here require no further action

The matrix in Figure 3.1 displays quadrants derived from two scales. It treats importance and attainment as scales rather than a set of disparate items, and it assumes that measures of central tendency can be calculated and have meaning.

The axes inside the figure represent the average score for attainment across all items and the average for importance determined in analogous manner. These in effect divide the space into four quadrants. The meaning of each quadrant is depicted in the figure. The average attainment and importance scores that an item receives allow the needs assessors to place the item number in an appropriate quadrant.

Above-average scores in importance and current status do not represent a need. When an item is above average in current status and below average in importance, the possibility exists for a cutback in resources. Why should there be expenditures in this case? There isn't any need when importance and current status are both below average. *Finally and most important,* being above average in importance and below average in current status fits the definition of need, and based on the survey data, it is one. The role of the needs assessor is to see which items fall into which quadrants. By placing their numbers in the appropriate quadrants the NAC and decision makers get a quick sense of where major discrepancies are located. Of course, there is the option of arbitrarily moving the horizontal and vertical standards to be more

Figure 3.1   The Quadrant Method

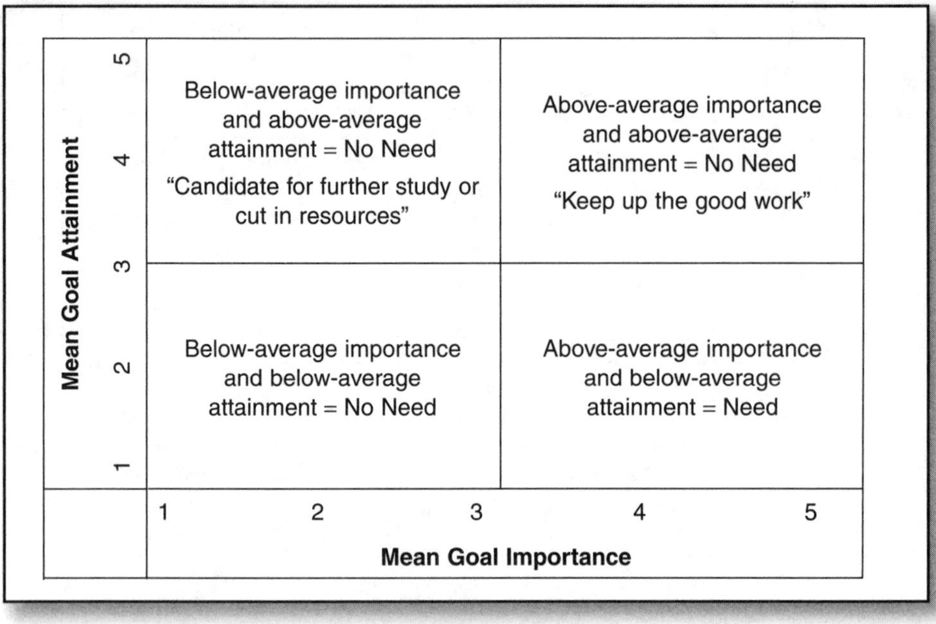

Note: The horizontal line bisecting the grid is the mean value for attainment from this particular sample, and its vertical counterpart is the mean for importance. The two lines can be arbitrarily adjusted to reduce or increase the numbers of items that would appear in the respective quadrants representing need.

selective in choosing need areas for further attention. If resources are extremely limited this might be the way to proceed.

This approach works best when items do not cluster together on the scales used. Unfortunately in needs assessment, most survey items are carefully preselected by the NAC and facilitator. In designing the survey, they were deemed to be of value for the study. Due to this, importance responses tend to be high with the cut score for importance losing much of its meaning. When this happens (which it frequently does), almost all variability in discrepancies comes from the current status part of the survey. The utility of the quadrant method depends on the nature of the data set, so examine it to see whether the method is suitable for the situation.

Satcher et al. (1980) demonstrated that identifying and understanding needs often cannot rely solely on two dimensions. Needs may be more complex, and prioritization may be premature without further probing and discussion by the NAC. In this regard, another example of triple scaling comes from preparedness training in public health. As part of funding requirements, training assessments in this field tend to be mandatory and generally focus on nine competencies often cited in the literature. An interesting triple-scaled approach is from a multistate project in Louisiana, Arkansas, Alabama, and Mississippi. Using a 5-point scale, Chauvin, Anderson, and Bowdish (2001) looked at frequency, self-confidence, and need for training. Table 3.8 is an excerpt of the results from their study for one competency area with five substatements.

Table 3.8   Triple Scaling for Competencies From Chauvin, Anderson, and Bowdish (2001) in Public Health

A. Describe the public health role in emergency response in a range of emergencies that might arise	Frequency?	Self-Confident?	Need Training?
"Uses surveillance protocols effectively"	A–B–C–D–E	A–B–C–D–E	A–B–C–D–E
"Uses appropriate investigation strategies"	A–B–C–D–E	A–B–C–D–E	A–B–C–D–E
"Determines and delivers public information appropriately"	A–B–C–D–E	A–B–C–D–E	A–B–C–D–E
"Coordinates and collaborates with internal agencies effectively"	A–B–C–D–E	A–B–C–D–E	A–B–C–D–E
"Coordinates and collaborates with external partners effectively"	A–B–C–D–E	A–B–C–D–E	A–B–C–D–E

Note: A = strongly disagree to E = strongly agree.

The competency area (labeled "A") is followed by the rating scales for the three dimensions: frequency of use, level of self-confidence, and need for training. There are several issues here. First, the choice of rating dimensions has to be made with respect to the respondent burden balanced against the information to be gained. In the Satcher et al. (1980) multiple-stakeholder survey, the gain from adding a feasibility scale outweighed the extra work on the part of the respondent. From that point, what constitutes a need and how it is defined will have to be determined by the NAC. After the need criterion is established (*a priori* by NAC discussion and/or *a posteriori* by looking over the data), the process becomes perfunctory in computing descriptive statistics, synthesizing the results, and finally prioritizing the observed discrepancies.

Another point about triple scaling needs to be mentioned in relation to interpretation. In the Chauvin et al. (2001) study, one would look for high frequency of a task being performed, low self-confidence, and high motivation for training. Those data would fit a "V"-shaped distribution (curve). The NAC or facilitator would plot the data and look for the Vs (the needs) as candidates for new initiatives and programs. Yet, a case could be made for items with a high frequency of occurrence, low self-confidence, and low motivation for training. It could be argued that they are needs as well, especially if the competencies are very critical. Obviously both patterns should be thoroughly considered by the NAC given local circumstances in making its final decision.

❖ PSYCHOMETRIC ANALYSES

NACs must additionally think about the psychometric properties of needs assessment instruments. Much like "fruit from the poison tree," poorly constructed instruments limit what can be determined from results while those of higher quality inspire greater faith in conclusions drawn from the data. For that reason, the needs assessor should examine the psychometric aspects of the measures used in the investigation. The essence of need is calculating a discrepancy score between what is and what should be. This requires sound measurements of the two conditions. In other words, are the "what is" and "what should be" scales reliable and valid? Are we comfortable that they have been measured well?

Reliability

An instrument is reliable when its items consistently yield similar results (Trochim & Donnelly, 2007). This can be determined by judgmental or statistical techniques. Sometimes with certain types of data this would be accomplished by checking on the consistency of multiple raters or observers. Take higher education where a number of outside experts conduct a review of course syllabi prior to a visit by an accrediting body. If four out of five reviewers believe the course content meets the threshold set by the accrediting body, observational data of this nature can be said to have an interrater agreement (reliability) of 80%.

When a needs assessment survey is administered twice to the same sample at different times and produces similar outcomes, it is test-retest reliable. This is not normally done since often there is only one opportunity to survey a sample. Internal consistency reliability, the most cited form, is a statistical technique to estimate the degree to which the items in the instrument if used again would lead to relatively the same results. Cronbach's (1951) alpha (an average of interitem correlations and the split-half technique (randomly splitting in half the items and correlating the two halves) are usually used. Alpha and split-half coefficients are easily computed using statistical software. Higher values for these calculations (going toward 1.0) indicate greater reliability and are based on the correlation of items with each other. Such values are commonly seen when a systematic process of developing surveys (see Book 3) is followed. Careful thought in wording items and making them as clear as possible leads to higher reliability.

Going beyond its use for reliability, a correlation matrix can be a valuable tool in scrutinizing survey data. Items that are highly correlated indicate that they are dealing with similar aspects of a variable, and low correlations are indicative of dissimilarity. This was the situation White, Altschuld, and Lee (2006a) encountered when they computed the correlation matrix for 11 items designed to measure the cultural aspects of minority college students in STEM retention programs. The reliability estimate for the 11 items was relatively low (.299) with many of them not strongly relating to each other leading to the low level of reliability. Based on the correlations found in Table 3.9, White et al. asked if there might be multiple aspects of culture embedded in the 11 items (more on this later). Asking questions like this point us to another facet of psychometric analysis, validity—that is, what are we really measuring?

Validity

An instrument is valid when it measures what it was designed to measure. There are a variety of ways by which the NAC can arrive at conclusions about the nature of instruments and scales embedded in them. Similar to reliability, some validity approaches are subjective, and others are statistical. The ways in which we get at validity vary and are determined by the type of data, level of facilitator expertise, context of the needs assessment, and parameters set by the NAC.

Table 3.9 Interitem Correlation Matrix

	Item_1	Item_2	Item_3	Item_4	Item_5	Item_6	Item_7	Item_8	Item_9	Item_10	Item_11
Item_1	1.00										
Item_2	.688	1.00									
Item_3	.524	.762	1.00								
Item_4	.221	.281	.233	1.00							
Item_5	.064	.167	.151	.063	1.00						
Item_6	.148	.247	.235	.189	.239	1.00					
Item_7	.305	.381	.385	.188	.170	.316	1.00				
Item_8	.409	.425	.367	.237	.222	.143	.414	1.00			
Item_9	.357	.309	.215	.293	.011	.160	.263	.470	1.00		
Item_10	.314	.343	.351	.202	.055	.101	.221	.321	.606	1.00	
Item_11	.291	.424	.429	.248	.141	.138	.258	.270	.407	.650	1.00

Face and content validity ascertain how well the instruments translate our concepts about needs into meaningful statements to which respondents supply answers and/or ratings (Trochim & Donnelly, 2007). For face validity do the items represent in clear and certain terms the topics being examined? On the "face of it" do they make sense to respondents? Content validity examines if the needs assessors have covered a full range of subtopics within the main topic such as the aforementioned public health competencies. These forms of validity rely on the judgment of individuals with expertise in the field and are often used in needs assessments. (Face and content validity additionally pertain to qualitative techniques such as focus group interviews, individual interviews, and observations.)

Criterion-related validity gauges the results of an instrument against preestablished criteria (Trochim & Donnelly, 2007). They are compared to those of a similar instrument found to measure the variable of interest (another reason for reviewing the literature). Predictive and convergent validity require the use of correlations to see how well the instrument performed. High correlation coefficients indicate the instrument was able to predict what it was proposed to predict or how well the results are comparable to those of other pertinent measures (Furr & Bacharach, 2008; Hopkins, 1998; Salkind, 2006). An example of this would be correlating employee job performance ratings with the supervisor's performance ratings.

Identifying Underlying Dimensions

Rather than validity, the concern of the NAC may be in understanding the different aspects that emerge from a needs assessment survey. These dimensions can be detected by means of more advanced statistical techniques like the exploratory factor analysis (EFA) White and colleagues (2006a) used when they uncovered subdimensions in the cultural values survey mentioned before. The EFA detected three different aspects of culture as well as the fact that some items should be omitted since they failed to have any importance in the analysis.

Instead of a one-dimensional survey, the instrument was measuring the features presented in Table 3.10: obligation to the community, responsibility to family and friends, and feeling about the academic program. Additionally, some of the items were more reliable than others. After signifying how the items grouped together, the EFA pointed toward those on which to focus the reliability statistics. For example, in Table 3.10, Items 1–3 clustered together and had a high reliability (coefficient of .852). The group containing Items 5 and 6 was far less reliable (.391), and the

Table 3.10 Psychometric Summary of Cultural Items

Item	Factor Loadings	Themes (Derived Variables) From the Items	Reliability
Item_1	.812	Sense of obligation to the community	.852
Item_2	.881		
Item_3	.818		
Item_5	.711	Sense of responsibility to family and friends	.391
Item_6	.761		
Item_9	.815	Feeling comfortable and confident in academic major	.790
Item_10	.856		
Item_11	.725		

third with Items 9–11 was a more reliable (.790) set. Missing from the table are Items 4, 7, and 8, which were deleted from the survey after the EFA suggested that they were not working as anticipated. In terms of utility, EFA and other factor analytic approaches are ways for the NAC to scrutinize the instrument moving beyond face validity to get at construct validity as just described. In assessments it may be very helpful to be aware of subdimensions (factors) in the data as well as how they might be perceived or rated by groups within the overall sample.

What is done statistically in any particular exploration of needs depends on the experience of the facilitator, the skills of the NAC, or those of a consultant. Whatever the case, a final caveat about reliability and validity is that they are subjective and objective determinations made about instruments. None will be perfectly valid or completely reliable (Stacey, 2005). That may not matter too much if the assessment is rich in methods and has data across sources that are highly corroborative.

❖ INFERENTIAL STATISTICS

Data collected from an assessment might be generalized to a population of potential consumers to test hypotheses about differences among groups or to examine relationships between variables. Inferential statistics would determine if observations from descriptive data might be in fact representative of real differences or relationships. Are the differences, if any, specific to a peculiar group? What types of relationships can be detected, and how strong are they? There are contexts in which inferential statistics are relevant in needs assessment.

They can be useful in ascertaining if the demographic characteristics found in the survey are akin to those for an entire service area. Then the NAC has greater assurance that the sample is truly representative, and this would be especially important for the epidemiological assessment of needs.

The within- and between-method variations presented in Book 1 and in Chapter 1 of this book can also be tested using inferential procedures. Within-method variations are those found in a data collection technique like a survey, which has similar questions but with slightly different wording for different groups (teachers, students, administrators, parents). Between-method variations relate to multiple ways of collecting data (focus groups, observations, etc.). In these situations it is important to determine whether the methods are yielding the same types of results or unique ones. If the results for the within- and between-method variations are the same, how the data were collected is not important. However, when one technique yields results statistically different than another, the question becomes why?

For example, consider the following situation from higher education. A tenure track faculty member was confronted with data obtained from student evaluations during a review by the departmental promotion and tenure committee. Based on a 5-point scale, the overall mean was approximately 4.00. The student commentaries, on the other hand, were laden with predominantly negative comments. How could the committee reconcile the differences between the two forms of data? Inferential procedures could be used with the scaled data to see if a trend emerged where the faculty member was making gains in the average student ratings. If the data permitted, it would be also interesting to know if there were subclassifications within the students who responded. Was the faculty member rated higher by one group than another based on class rank or academic major? Is there evidence of trends in the student ratings when examined longitudinally? Inferential statistics can be used to reveal the subtle nuances in the data that may be otherwise hidden.

This same dynamic occurs in needs assessment practice within large organizations. Differences may be detected at the corporate office in one part of the country and not be found at other locations. This is common in large health care organizations where the delivery of services is influenced by regional factors—so much so that what works at "corporate" may not at another location. In other words, one approach may not always work with everyone.

❖ DISCREPANCY SCORES

After ensuring the quality of scales, discrepancy scores are determined. Because we typically are working with a large number of items, we might create composites by averaging related items and even checking on the psychometric properties of the composites. In the Chauvin et al. (2001) study of public health preparedness, one composite area, Importance of Computer Training, was comprised of key statements rated on a five-point scale. Chauvin et al. were able to provide empirical evidence that the composites were in fact reliable and valid.

To get a sense of how this is done, see Table 3.11, which contains the average responses for four individuals. At the bottom of each column each respondent has an average score. At the end of each row a composite score for each item has been computed. Further, all of the items have been averaged, thus creating an overall score for the cluster of items. While cluster averages are useful for discrepancies, they may mask

Table 3.11   Table of Composite Scores

Software/hardware training importance	Subj_1	Subj_2	Subj_3	Subj_4	Mean
Training in software diagnosis	1	1	5	5	3.00
Training in PC troubleshooting	1	3	4	2	2.50
Training in installing new software	1	1	1	2	1.25
Training in installing new hardware	4	5	5	5	4.75
Average training need (per respondent and cluster)	1.75	2.50	3.75	3.50	2.88

Note: Based on 5-point scale.

valuable information, which require a closer look. In Table 3.11 the average software/hardware training score (2.88) is slightly skewed toward agreement. Upon closer inspection, most respondents indicate that a greater value (4.75) was attained for installing new hardware. The cluster score was hiding the effect of specific items contributing to it. Be alert to such possibilities when working with data.

❖ CORRELATION AND REGRESSION
IN NEEDS ASSESSMENT DATA

Besides being used to check the quality of the instrument, correlations reflect the nature and strength of relationships between variables. Some of these analyses can be statistically complex, but there are basic applications in needs assessment. As a case in point, it would be helpful to know how many hours of training are needed to obtain a minimum level of proficiency. Or, in an educational setting, it would help to know the number of study hours needed for a passing grade. Correlation allows the needs assessor to do this. The best way to start is to plot the relationship between the variables such as Lee et al. (2007a) did in their needs assessment of college students. They collected data on two variables—importance to academic success and satisfaction with the service. From the plot it was clear that there was a positive relationship: As academic success increases, satisfaction increases. The next step was computing the correlation coefficient, Pearson's coefficient ($r = .298$), which indicated a slight to moderate relationship between the variables. Correlations may be positive or negative, and the strength of the relationship is indicated by size going from 0 = no relationship to 1.0 = perfect relationship (or a one-to-one match).

Another concern here is how much satisfaction was due to importance. Squaring the r is the way to do this, and it revealed that while about 9% of satisfaction was a function of the importance students placed on the service, 91% was due to something else. By analogy the needs assessor could look at other factors (quality of experiences in academic programs, availability of supportive services, social environments, etc.) in relation to satisfaction to see if they contribute to understanding needs. Even though correlation and regression statistics can be tricky to work with (see the many texts on the topic such as Mertler & Vanatta, 2005; Meyers, Gamst, & Guarino, 2006; Pedhazur, 1997; Stevens, 2007; and Warner, 2008), the key point is that relationships among variables can be insightful for the NAC.

❖ OTHER QUANTITATIVE DATA

While surveys have been the main focus so far, most of the analytical strategies would apply to a good portion of the data from archival records, observations, databases, and so forth. The challenge with any analysis is interpreting and presenting the results in a fashion that will be meaningful to a diverse group of decision makers and stakeholders. Overuse of statistical jargon can lead to disinterested audiences or the inability of the NAC to act on the recommendations.

The principles about designing survey instruments, sampling, checking psychometric properties, analyzing the results, and deriving meaningful information for needs assessment purposes generalize to other forms of quantitative data. One type would be in accessible community databases. A community research agency in central Ohio (Community Research Partners, 2005) created a database of various indicators about the local community. It is available to those who want to learn about the community or wish to study specialized concerns and issues (housing, poverty, health care, available resources, etc.). Most of the data come from census reports and other similar sources and are assumed to be reliable and valid. Of course, the reliability and validity of a source must always be looked at in regard to the instruments and collection mechanisms from which the data are derived.

Certainly from the database, comparisons of subgroups can and will be made by users. No new data are required for such endeavors, recognizing that the information is limited to what is in the base and may have to be supplemented by interviews and observations. It is recommended that any database analysis be accompanied by such qualitative procedures.

In a similar vein is a federally funded project currently underway that is aimed at creating a guide for states to assess vocational rehabilitation needs (Stockdill & Kraus, 2009) and to do subsequent planning in accord with the discrepancies found. While parts of a needs assessment in this area may require that new data be created, a significant amount comes from existing national and regional archives and records broken down in ways that would be relevant to a particular state or to localized vicinities within it. This approach to assessing needs is flexible, adaptable, and quite utilitarian. The project provides descriptions of census reports, Social Security information, national community surveys, and so forth and demonstrates how the data can be used in a state context. Needs assessors should conduct brief searches for products like the two above before getting into their specific assessments.

Looking more closely at vocational rehabilitation, what are the analysis principles that apply? First, again, is the notion of subgroups of the population nested in the data. In terms of rehabilitation one has to think about the total nationwide population in regard to ethnicities and age disparities in a specific state and different locations within it. The rates and sizes of needs probably have significant variation by subgroups and areas. Tables could be prepared to show such aspects of needs. Inferential statistics can be employed to see if there are significant differences between national and state populations, and other testing could be done for more drilled-down aspects of the population.

If significance is observed and the actual differences are of substance, that will be important for considering what the actual needs are, what the priorities might be, which among many needs should be resolved, and where precious resources should be placed for maximum benefit. Coupled with these analyses would be information from the rehabilitation services actually provided in local areas. Some of this might come from other databases or other, somewhat different kinds of data.

The Rehabilitation Services Act of 1973 (Public Law 93–112) requires all vocational rehabilitation providers to collect information on individuals being served. The data set includes a variety of demographic characteristics and what services are being made available and used, who is utilizing them, how successful they are, and how insights gained from this information might be juxtaposed with the previous data to determine where resources should be focused. Again, simple needs assessment data might not be that simple, especially when they have to be blended into a meaningful whole.

Another principle drawn from survey analysis is in relation to examining and verifying the quality of data. In most cases the national and state information from databases is accepted as being accurate and representing a reasonable picture of the population and subgroups. There are exceptions, so don't blindly be accepting, but keep in mind that many of the indicators in them are fairly standardized. Agency data might be a little more suspect and would require checking to ensure it is reliable and valid. This would entail more costs in assessing needs. NACs should to some degree think about whether funds should be invested for such purposes.

Beyond that a word of caution is necessary on this topic particularly in terms of vocational rehabilitation but applicable to many fields. Human needs are dynamic and subject to economic and other forces. To fully understand them it may be necessary to examine the micro and macro trends that are taking place in the environment along with other data to determine program and policy needs. What is taking place in the business sector? Are technological changes creating or reducing job opportunities? What are the prospects for the economy, and what are projected needs for workers? How strong or weak is the job market? How acquainted are those providing rehabilitation services and those receiving them with some of these factors? To what extent are people not only knowledgeable about the issues but consciously incorporating them into thinking about personal and organizational needs? Are sound policies being developed at the state level, and are they focused enough to lead to meaningful decisions?

Moving to yet another field, public health, considerable use is made of the survey technique and databases in a manner akin to what was described for vocational rehabilitation. In 2006, a group of evaluators working in state centers for public health preparedness compiled an overview of needs assessment procedures used in the field (Centers for Public Health Preparedness Network of Evaluators, 2006). It was done by the evaluators with assistance from ASPH (Association of Schools of Public Health).

The overview contains an analysis of key features of needs assessments cutting across 15 states and a brief synopsis of their instrumentation and methodology as pertinent. Some general observations drawn from the compilation are that some states were able to tie the assessments into decision making; extensive double scaling in surveys was noted; scales dealt with a variety of topics such as competence, preferred training topics, satisfaction with training, and so on; generally only one rather than multiple methods could be used due to cost factors; surveys were administered to diverse groups; Web and "snail mail" administration was employed to distribute surveys; discrepancy analysis where feasible was carried out; and stakeholder involvement from the beginning of the conceptualization of the process through later parts was apparent.

Surveys took a variety of forms. In one state they consisted of a very lengthy inventory of supplies and resources available in localities for disasters (natural calamities such as earthquakes, floods, epidemics, and terrorist attacks). Given the length and detailed nuances of the instrument, this would be a case where concerns about validity and reliability would be high. In numerous other states the surveys focused on the self-perceived competencies of job incumbents to handle preparedness situations and needs for training.

In another state there was an interesting study comparing and contrasting different geographic areas, and by this means public health resource needs could be identified. This was mostly done through existing records. When broken down in terms of population density (urban, suburban, or rural), the ability of different locations to respond to public health preparedness needs was discernable. Subgroup averages were studied, and inferences were made as to what resources might be needed. The means from the entire sample in different categories of resources were the standards or norms by which to examine if individual locations seemed to be deficient. Results could also be examined in relation to national standards.

Reiterating, most of the content of this chapter relied on surveys to explain how to analyze needs assessment data, but the concepts fit other forms of data. The essential idea is what we can identify and learn about needs from the information we collect.

❖ CONCLUSIONS FROM NUMERICAL DATA

After analyzing the quantitative data, another question arises: "How important are the results?" When something is statistically significant, it does not necessarily mean the results have practical value. Will they be viewed as important by consumers, providers, decision makers, and other stakeholders in the needs assessment context? Numbers are always valuable, but there may be too much faith placed on them and not enough on practical aspects or a more comprehensive picture of needs (Moore, 2006). To that end Patten (2009) provided five considerations for determining the practical aspects of statistical significance.

The first is the *cost-effectiveness* of the finding. What benefit will result from it and at what cost? Computer-assisted technology, for example, is frequently found to enhance organizational performance but at what startup, training, maintenance, and long-term upgrade cost? Are the costs worth it? Sometimes it may be more cost-effective or utilitarian to hire additional personnel. This means that at some point the NAC will have to consider the financial implications of results from the assessment.

Second, does implementing the statistical findings make a *crucial difference?* Large samples in surveys may detect small differences. Do they really make a difference to the organization? How many people are actually affected by or involved with a discrepancy? Is the number of sufficient size to impact our decision making? What about a large need for a smaller group versus a lesser need for a much larger number of people?

Next is *stakeholder acceptability.* Will the results be accepted by the constituents because, if not, it isn't likely that they will lead to change? This takes us back to work early in Phase II (Books 1 and 2) when we made choices of instruments and methods. Did we choose well and in accord with the information needs of the organization and what its key personnel attend to or would attract their attention?

The above principle goes hand-in-hand with the fourth consideration, *public and political acceptability.* Stem cell research is a prime example of how need and capability may not be enough. Until there is adequate public and political support, little will come from the findings, and moreover little will be done.

Finally, what are the *ethical and legal concerns?* Regardless of benefit or reduced cost, sometimes it may not be ethical (or legal) to act on the results. It is unethical and illegal to withhold services in public health, social welfare, and education settings based on differences such as gender, socioeconomic status, race/ethnicity, and so forth. Another example is withholding information on the side effects of drug regimens. Behind all the numbers are real human beings. It is sort of like unemployment numbers in that they are just that until unhappily you become unemployed and then the situation takes on a whole different meaning. We must not forget that the numbers come from the trials and tribulations of real individuals.

❖ SUMMARY OF THE STEPS FOR
   QUANTITATIVE DATA ANALYSIS

The steps for analyzing quantitative needs assessment data presented in this chapter and a brief summary of the details pertaining to them are outlined in Table 3.12.

Table 3.12   Steps for Analyzing Quantitative Data

Step	Commentary
Data collection	Compiling the data for manual analysis or electronic entry into spreadsheets or computer software
Data quality	Visual inspection to ensure the quality and integrity of the data prior to analyses
Data manipulation	Treatment of the data including making backup copies, dividing them into subsets, restructuring them, and transforming them into the format(s) needed for the analyses
Data analysis	Analyzing the data via (a) descriptive statistics with tables and graphs, (b) inspection of the psychometric quality (reliability and validity) of the instrument, and (c) inferential statistics to test hypotheses
Data summary	Summarizing results of the statistical analyses in a manner that the consumers (NAC, stakeholders, etc.) can understand and use

Highlights of the Chapter

1. The importance of how data were collected and structured for numerical analysis was underscored.

2. Numerous concerns were raised about ensuring the quality (reliability and validity) of the scales used in needs assessment.

3. Visual inspections of the data received stress throughout the discussion and were seen as necessary for becoming enmeshed in the data and their analysis.

4. Various ideas to guide analysis such as describing participants; summarizing responses using frequencies, means, and variances; discrepancy indicators; creating composite scores; and looking at relationships among variables were offered.

5. Practical principles and discussion of same were embedded in the text for coming to judgments about statistical results. Backing away from the results and judging them in terms of key principles would be meaningful for all needs assessments.

4

Getting the Results
Together for Prioritization

❖ SOME FIRST CONSIDERATIONS

Now we are further into the nitty-gritty of needs assessment. The focus appropriately shifts to presenting the results to decision-making groups. The qualitative and quantitative data have been analyzed, and the needs assessment committee (NAC) has a good sense of what the primary needs are, what they look like, their size, and how many individuals are affected. Starting with a larger number of needs they have been winnowed into a much smaller, more important subset. In this respect the assessment may seem easier to complete. This is all fine, but there probably are, especially in a large-scale assessment, still too many needs to deal with based on a complex, multimethods picture. The effort has been solid, but the data and findings have to be put in a coherent format for decision making.

Some of the data are numeric and lend themselves to determining discrepancies whereas the qualitative sources are more subjective representing feelings, perceptions, attitudes, and values. It is necessary to collate everything into a comprehensive portrayal of needs and factors related to them. This will help the NAC and others arrive at priorities from the rich pool of information that has been obtained.

A logical way to do this is to organize the results from each source into an array ordered from the strongest (highly indicated) to the weakest needs. Then compare across sources to see the degree of agreement or disagreement. What stands out, what seems to have the strongest endorsement (from each method), what needs have the greatest consensus (buy-in), and so forth? At times this may be difficult to do. Demarest, Holey, and Leatherman (1984) used three methods to determine needs for hospital-based nurses and found that, although there was some overlap, for the most part there were noticeable differences in the needs observed.

But let us note that in many efforts we don't project results similar to those of Demarest et al. (1984). If records, interviews, and surveys were used, the NAC would attend to the needs that are prominent across the sources. This would be a key piece of information for the group's deliberation about what to recommend to the organization. If data from multiple constituencies were obtained and pointed toward the same needs, the arguments in favor of them are strengthened. As in the game of bridge, corroboration across numerous sources constitutes a long suit and a strong hand.

A second scenario would be support for needs that are highly rated in two out of three sources without support or contradiction from the third. This line of thought could easily be extended into more scenarios (see Table 4.1).

Table 4.1   Guidelines for Treating Needs Assessment Data From Multiple Sources

Guideline	Principle	Discussion
Data Fit Together	Data from all sources are in agreement regarding a need	Best of all situations—the data provide corroboration
Data Mostly Fit	Data from key sources are in agreement with no contradictory evidence	Fairly good situation especially since there is no contradictory evidence
Data Point to Different Needs	Either different methods or different constituencies are indicating diverse needs but not ones necessarily in opposition to each other	Not as desirable as above but not necessarily bad if there are logical reasons for differences or one source is better implemented than another
Data in Opposition	Data are contradictory to a need (e.g., parents and teachers radically disagreeing on emphases in science textbooks)	Worst case especially if the collection methods are all well implemented—probably will require obtaining more data or more investigation

Caution is in order here. The methods might not be of equal quality, and as a consequence some information may be of lesser importance. To illustrate, suppose a good quality survey had provided valid and reliable information. The questions were clear and in depth, with substantial item completion rates and high returns from multiple constituencies. An appropriate analysis had been conducted with indices of need based on discrepancy scores, and rank-ordering of needs showed a general consensus for all groups surveyed.

In the same assessment a second source consisted of open-ended interviews with a few key informants (representatives of groups who could offer insights into the mind-sets of their constituencies) or a very selective sample. The data did not provide discrepancies but were informative and provided some different perspectives than the survey results. In this case a concern arises about how to think through the two outcomes from the distinct data collection mechanisms. In our view, more faith should be placed on the survey and the order of needs it produced, with less weight assigned to the interviews. If the interview process was larger and generated consistent results, its credibility would be enhanced. This situation might lead the NAC to consider doing a focus group interview (FGI) or a few more individual interviews to resolve different viewpoints if they arose.

Multiple sources are like this. They have varying levels of how they have been administered, may use different samples, and often are based on unique questions and epistemological premises. The data generated may not be comparable. Thus in every multiple-methods endeavor, the NAC must judge the integrity and strength of each source and perhaps place more emphasis on one and less on another. This raises concerns:

- Does the sample size seem reasonable for the inferences drawn from the data?

- What groups were involved in the methods, and to what extent can the results be contrasted and/or compared?

- Were there any problems (survey return rates by some groups, failure to get the right individuals to attend the FGI, etc.)?

- How might the problems affect the quality of the information received?

- How good were the questions used to guide observations, interviews, and other techniques?

- Are the results from some sources more compelling? If so, why?

- What are additional considerations?

The NAC should allot time to discuss data quality before creating its summary of results and deriving recommendations. Generally it will be easy for the group to achieve consensus regarding the value and quality of different methods.

❖ WEIGHTING RESPONSES FOR PRIORITIZATION

The last issue is about responses from multiple constituencies, especially in survey work. Suppose a survey has been administered to high school students, teachers, and parents. Compared with students and parents, teachers report a much larger number of discrepancies on certain items. One way to go about calculating an overall discrepancy is to treat each group as being of equal weight for the need area. This fits well with the concept of democracy in that all input is equally important and valid. There should be uniform weights of 1 with no group differentiation. Average "what is," "what should be," and discrepancy scores are calculated using 3 (in this case) as the denominator.

But an alternative argument could be that in any new or changed school programs the teachers will have to do the work. They are the Level 2 individuals who deliver services and implement changes. The ultimate success of any solution strategy mainly falls to them. Service providers ultimately make or break a new program. If they perceive a larger discrepancy, then their opinion should receive greater attention in needs-based decision making; their opinions and ratings should count more. If this seems reasonable, why not give their responses a weight of 2 or 3 and the other groups' responses weights of 1? (Indeed one of the criteria in Sork's [1998] procedure for prioritizing is adult learning, undoubtedly based on the concept that adults within organizations are the main implementers of change and new/altered procedures. If they don't buy in, the likelihood of success is greatly diminished. See Books 1 and 3 in the KIT.)

Let's make this more complicated conceptually. It is probable that there will be different numbers of respondents among the constituencies. We should describe the discrepancy score for each group, compare these scores, and then calculate an overall discrepancy with equal weights. But this does not take into consideration that different sample sizes contribute to each of the discrepancy scores. If one group is larger, it could be argued that its members' opinion should have a greater impact on the final discrepancy. Students will be the largest group in most school-based needs assessments. So why not include sample size in our calculations? It would affect the overall discrepancies across groups for items and have an impact on the highest-priority needs. Obviously there are options for what seems so straightforward on first glance.

What to do is not automatic since there are many subtle choices available. The NAC and facilitator could do the calculations several ways to see the degree to which they differ or are similar. Would one set of results affect subsequent choices in a certain way? Would another lead to an alternative direction? Perhaps the various results could be shared with the decision-making groups. Raising these issues may cause more hackles than it's worth (see Example 4.1). On the other hand, needs do result in actions that affect organizations, individuals in them, and groups in major ways.

Example 4.1

Don't Fool With Those Weights!

One of the authors was teaching needs assessment to rural school guidance counselors in statewide workshops throughout the United States. In such settings he proposed that discrepancy data collected from students, parents, teachers, and guidance counselors be differentially weighted since the latter would have to implement any new or modified programs in career development for rural students. Much effort might be involved, and certainly the counselors should have a bigger voice in decisions that affect their jobs and work environment. They have unique understandings from which to view counseling issues in schools and the problems students express to them.

Instead of having group weights of 1, the author suggested that the data be calculated with the counselor scores having weights of 2 or 3 with unity for the other groups. The rationale was as given above.

Was that ever the wrong way to go! Talk about almost getting hooted out of the room! The idea was totally and quickly rejected in the three workshops in which it was proposed. Instinctively, it just violated the notion that we live in a democracy, especially where schools and children are the focus and that fact should be paramount in our examination of issues. Everyone's opinion counts, and one group should not dominate. What may make logical sense would tend to be going against the grain of the American fabric especially as brought up in a public forum.

Yet, remember the outcomes of assessment may require serious changes in how work is done and have an impact on the lives of those delivering services, not only those who are recipients of them. Should we not, at least to some degree and for speculative purposes, look at the data in several ways? Doing so will challenge what groups think about and perhaps encourage them to see the perspectives of Level 2 in greater detail. Whichever side of the issue you as a needs assessor or NAC fall on, this is another dimension of the enterprise.

❖ PORTRAYING THE DATA

Returning to how to put data from multiple methods and sources together and portray it for prioritization, several approaches noted in the literature are described. The first is the use of goal attainment scores (GAS) for a project in Nashville. Another was applied in an evaluation/needs assessment context with a national organization. A brief discussion of each follows.

Goal Attainment Scores (GAS)

The essence of this concept is a derived scaling approach that begs the question of why it would be used in place of the actual scales that were employed. Ordinarily when doing an assessment, the idea is to focus the playing field so that you are not looking at a tremendously wide spectrum of areas. If you don't, groups can quickly dissipate and lose direction. The workload gets too large, and enthusiasm soon wanes.

Some assessments tend to get broad in scope as is often the case in education and social services. Another thing that happens even when scope is limited is that other areas of concern will crop up during the process. This was pointed out when Witkin and Altschuld (1995) suggested that when this kind of information appears it should be noted but tabled for later use by the organization. Do not deal with it in any detail to avoid diluting the emphasis on the concern(s) in consideration at the present time.

This way of thinking is seen in Figure 4.1. While departmental assessment was the central concern, schoolwide problems and gaps arose in the study. They were recorded but tabled for later review. The microscope was solely on within-department issues. This is taken into consideration in the figure with the label "hold for systemwide NA [needs assessment]." The facilitator should be aware of these and be prepared to document their occurrence without letting them get in the way of the problems of immediate concern.

No matter how much the NAC and the facilitator try to focus the assessment, the school and/or community could insist that a broader look at needs is required using multiple methods across constituencies. As a result a process is undertaken to look at needs in various aspects of a high school—mathematics, science, language, health, social studies, English, and second-language instruction with input from teachers, administrators, parents, the community, and students.

The district sees a survey with separate sections for the different areas of the curriculum as the way to go. There would be 8–10 double- or

Figure 4.1 Flow of Events in Phase I, Based on Issues in a Departmental System

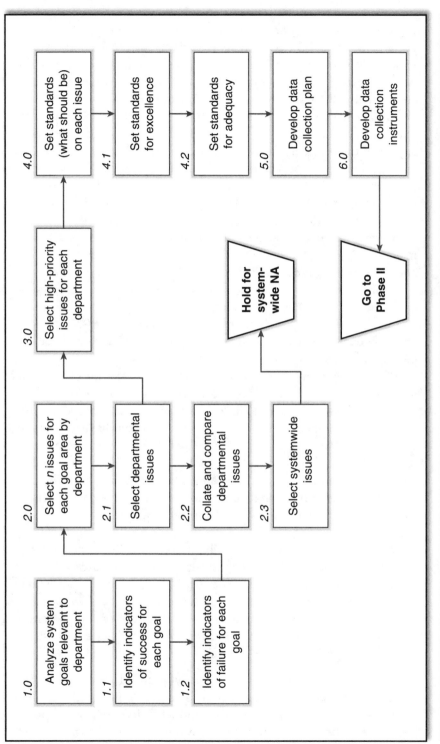

Source: From Witkin, B. R. & Altschuld, J. W. (1995). *Planning and conducting needs assessment.* Thousand Oaks, CA: Sage Publications.

67

triple-scaled items per area with two of the scales being "what should be" and "what is." Other methods would include focus group or individual interviews and an examination of testing data covering a period of time. This is an illustration of a multimethod, multiconstituent assessment with possibly between- and within-method variations.

In this scenario the complexity of the needs assessment has dramatically escalated. The cost of the effort is substantial, but the board approved the necessary funds. (Note that in the prior chapter this kind of scenario was not observed in national data from public health preparedness due to the increased financial requirements for such studies.) So everything is implemented, and now the question is what to do with the array of data that have been collected. How are they to be handled and presented in a manner that will lead to sensible decision making? How can we make sense of the data, and what would be a good mechanism to display them for decision-making audiences?

Embedded in these questions are things like how to compare discrepancies from mathematics with those in learning a second language and what to do with the data from different methods. It isn't immediately evident how to juxtapose them and come up with meaning. Can we generate a scale that permits comparison and at the same time doesn't lose too much information? Are we willing to let go of some of the detail to arrive at choices and ultimate directions for the organization?

GAS allows us to do this. This is its advantage, but embedded in the process of creating GAS there is a weakness. Trade-offs have to be made, and are we willing to consciously make them? There are numerous content areas for scrutiny, and students in the district are not doing well in a number of them. Somehow the available resources have to be directed toward one; there isn't enough money for all of them. Hard choices have to be made. Here is how it might be approached.

> *Step 1*: Decide on the scale to be used. It might be as simple as where 1 represents no evidence supportive of the area as a need from a particular data source up to a 5, which would indicate there is strong, compelling support for the need. Points 2–4 would obviously go from low to high but would not be on the extremes. Although a 5-unit range is not mandatory (others are possible), let's stay with 5 for sake of argument.

> *Step 2*: As a group (the NAC usually would do the GAS work), think about what would constitute evidence from a source about a need. That is a curious statement, and what does it mean? Suppose we were looking at mathematics. Examine the results from survey questions about the topic.

What discrepancies are there?

Are they similar across different groups that have taken the survey?

Or is there more of a mixed pattern with some items (or subsets) on the survey being agreed upon and others not?

Do we consider a small gap in certain types of mathematics large and meaningful, and what is guiding our thought processes?

What features of the data stand out as being strong and/or weak?

Are we sure enough in our convictions to justify our views of the data that would be defensible to others in the organization?

From these deliberations the NAC reaches a decision about the strength of the data in support of a need or a subset of needs if it seems best to break them down into a smaller grouping of items. At that point agreement must be reached as to what value (scale point) to use for the GAS that characterizes the level of support from the data source.

What is critical to the process is that there should be discussion of what might be a 5, what might be a 1, and gradations in between. To facilitate such deliberations the facilitator of the assessment might develop an example or a brief exercise for the committee to get a sense of the rating process. It should include the size of the discrepancy, how many people are in need, and how important it might seem to the organization. The exercise probably should avoid going to the solution side of needs and keep attention on intrinsic value.

Step 3: Remember that there are numerous subject matter areas in our survey, records have been analyzed, and in-depth qualitative information has been collected and summarized. What has to be done next is to apply the same kind of logic as described above. The results will have to have values assigned from 1 to 5 in analogous fashion for all sources in an area (say, mathematics), and then the same would be done for social studies, second-language learning, and so forth across the data sources.

It is important to emphasize that all NAC members should go through similar training in regard to providing numerical values. There is need for everyone doing ratings to have the same mind-set (to be on the same page) about the procedure; otherwise problems could arise with the worst being acrimonious disagreement in the group.

Step 4: With training and understanding, the NAC or subgroups as desired can be given the task of coming up with ratings for how each source does or doesn't support a particular needs candidate. This tends to work well if each member of the group does this independently. Doing so avoids groupthink, and if results are generally in agreement it adds credence to the outcome.

Simple forms might be made up that have a place for the rater's name, the score, and some notes about why he or she saw that score as appropriate. The sheets would be useful for discussion purposes and would serve as a record for later use if the scores were challenged. The sheets may be consulted if there are disagreements or to confirm the basis upon which a rating was given.

Step 5: The last activity is one where the data are arrayed in a format that facilitates decision making. In 1996, Wilson, Shayne, Lipsey, and Derzon came up with a clever way to do this. They developed a table where the need areas were denoted by rows and the columns represented the sources of data. In the cells they used symbols and a variation of a bar graph to show the scores obtained for each source. Or, one could simply have the numeric value for the source in the cell, but bar graphs are more visually appealing. A version of such a table (Table 4.2) is provided.

Table 4.2 Indicators of Need-Service Gaps for Different Service Areas

Service Areas	Private Nonprofit Community Services■	Public Community Services■
Child care	▦▦▦▦□□□□■■■■■	▦▦▦▦■■■■
Housing assistance & shelter	▦▦▦▦□□□□■■■■■	▦▦▦▦■■■
Adult day care & home care	▦▦▦□□□□□▪▪▪▪▫	▦▦▦□□□
Service for abuse, neglect, & domestic violence	▦▦▦▦□□□□■■■	▦▦▦■
Nutrition, food, meals	▦▦▦□□□□□■■■	▦▦▦■■■■
Transportation	▦▦▦□□□□■■■■	▦▦▦■■■
Employment services	▦▦▦□□□□■■■■	▦▦▦■■■
Mental health & counselling services	▦▦▦□□□□■■■■	▦▦▦■■
Parent support services	▦▦▦▦□□□■■■	▦▦▦▦■■■

Service Areas	Private Nonprofit Community Services■	Public Community Services■
Legal assistance	⊠⊠□□□□□■■■	⊠⊠■■
Life skills and remedial education	⊠⊠⊠□□□■■■■	■□□■■
Support services for disabilities	⊠⊠⊠□□□■■■■	⊠⊠⊠■
Financial & emergency assistance	⊠⊠⊠⊠□□□■■	⊠⊠⊠⊠■■■■
Foster care & adoption	■□□■□□■■■■	■□□■
Substance abuse prevention & treatment	⊠⊠⊠□□□□■	⊠⊠⊠■■■
Health care support services	⊠⊠⊠□□□■	⊠⊠⊠■■■
Social & recreational activities	■□□■□□■■	■□□■■
Pregnancy prevention & maternity	⊠⊠□□■	⊠⊠■■
Immigration support services	⊠□□■	■□□

■Longer bars reflect larger need-service gaps

⊠ = Community Perceptions (same values used for both private nonprofit and public services)

□ = Financial resources (available only for private nonprofit services)

■ = Service Capacity (separate indicators for private nonprofit and public services)

▨ = Estimated from partial data

Source: Wilson et al. (1996). Used by permission.

Going through a process of creating GAS is easily carried out by the NAC. It has the advantage of creating a simple and communicative table of results. Its utility is in how quickly the NAC can see what the most supported areas of need might be and can situate all needs on a common metric even when they are from different content areas such as in the educational scenario guiding the discussion. It is this last feature that enhances its allure for portraying data from multiple sources in a condensed manner.

Unfortunately, good things usually have drawbacks. First, the scores are derived or transformed and somewhat distant from their point of origination. Judgment has gone into generating them, and they may not convey the same meaning suggested by the original data. Assigning a numeric value to interviews is not the same thing as an in-depth examination of quantitative results or doing the same to carefully developed themes coming from qualitative methods. And at other times, a derived score for a quantitative variable may not carry the same conviction and force as one for open-ended data or vice versa (see Table 4.2).

A second concern is something that was almost silently slipped into the creation of the new scores for the educational areas. Notice a value of 5 assigned to mathematics that was derived from a review of the records might come from a different stance than the same value in social studies. For example, a math test score gap of one half of a standard deviation below the mean (or some kind of effect size) might be given a 5 whereas three quarters of a standard deviation in social studies might command the same 5 rating. When comparing the two the nuance is hidden and lost unless made explicit in deliberations. Some knowledge (which could be important in decision making) has been sacrificed, and subtle judgments have been made to simplify the data and render them into a usable format and structure.

By the same token, it is possible to get mired down in all the data and become so overwhelmed that it becomes difficult to deal with the multitude of findings. Factors such as the complexity of the decision-making situation, the nature of the data, the methods (number, type) employed, and the constituencies from which the data were obtained all have bearing on whether GAS or a fuller portrayal is warranted. In Table 4.3, several basic ways of presenting data are profiled.

Table 4.3   Ways of Presenting Needs Assessment Data From Multiple Sources

Features	Goal Attainment Scores (GAS)	Short Summaries per Source	Collated Summary Across Sources
Outcome	One-page table that is very good for decision making	Set of short (1- to 2-page) sheets per each major source of data or in some instances per subgroup/ constituency	A large, somewhat complex table generated from the one-page summaries
Ease of construction	Relatively easy	Relatively easy although more interpretation and write-up of the data are required	A little more difficult but still fairly easy, but table will take some time to prepare

Features	Goal Attainment Scores (GAS)	Short Summaries per Source	Collated Summary Across Sources
Abstraction from original data	Large degree of abstraction	Closest to original source, preserves much of the meaning in and sense of the data	Some abstraction, but a degree of the original data is maintained though not as much as in the short summaries
Ease of use	Very good in this regard—information is available at a glance	Generally good but takes more reading and interpretation especially if there are contradictory indications for a need	In between GAS table and the use of short summaries
Cautions	While in some respects using GAS is the best way to go, much detail and feel for context of the data will disappear by going to a common metric	The best set of information, but this approach is confounded by the fact that more and more detail can make decision making somewhat harder to accomplish	Although this is a collation of the short summaries, it can lead to a fairly heavy one- or two-page table with perhaps some difficulty in use for decision making
Overall comments	The loss of the context and meaning of especially the qualitative data may be too great; it all depends on the decisions to be made and the nature of the organizational milieu	It may be wise at times to deal with more of the subtleties in the data, for important budget and action choices will have to be made	In some respects the best option because a portion of the flavor of the data is retained; remember the table may be more difficult to construct

Let's turn to the collation of data approaches represented in the last columns of the table. They seem to be more appropriate when the choices for action reflect serious investments of resources, tend to be disruptive to the organization, and are in relation to major changes in the way things are done. Here more summarized data as opposed to abstraction would be necessary for selecting options and communicating with key personnel in the organization. The trick is to have enough data for guidance and explanation without engulfing and overwhelming the needs assessment. A delicate balance is the goal.

Short Summaries per Source

This may be the best way of portraying data. It forces the needs assessors and the NAC to deal with the information and results in a thoughtful manner as to what the data are saying and their meaning. As you do this it is important to reflect on the fact that data are collected primarily during Phases I and II and only sometimes in Phase III. Summaries should be generated for all sources rather than just for Phase II. Phase I, for instance, might include information from scans of the literature and/or the environment, analysis of records, reports completed by the organization or other groups, transcripts from discussions in group meetings, and a few group or individual interviews that have been conducted.

Each source should have a brief summary of its results as follows.

Step 1: Treat each method separately as much as possible. Try not to contaminate the results from one with those of another. Divide the NAC into teams with each having responsibility for the condensation of what was learned from the single method as independently as possible.

The facilitator of the process should instruct the teams about how to construct the summaries. Stress should be placed on not thinking about what has been collected from other sources. The teams should try to wear metaphorical blinders.

Step 2: Provide categories to guide the teams as they create their summaries. The categories might go something like this:
- the nature of the method in a paragraph or short phrases (teams should be consistent in generating this part of the summary);
- main findings supportive of the need in the area of concern;
- any evidence that might be contradictory to the main findings in support of the need (sections of a survey did not seem to be as anticipated, there were subgroups in the sample that were less than enthusiastic about the proposition, open-ended

comments on the survey were much different in tone than expected, etc.); and

- findings that are neither supportive nor contradictory but are worthy of the NAC's attention or potential consideration (such as a novel idea).

In the last section of the summary, the team might also judge how well a method was implemented. All parts of the summary should be labeled as suggested above and be in short phrases as much as the team can generate results this way. The facilitator might prepare a sample to guide team members. The idea is to have, in abbreviated form, the main things coming out of the data from a source. The results are being put into a format that enables a group to quickly see what a source has told it. Very rapidly group members can compare and contrast information from sources.

Step 3: Assign results obtained from different methods to the teams. Each team member should work independently before all members get back together to produce a collective summary. If subgroups and/or quite different constituencies have been involved in the effort, make sure that results per group are recorded on the short summaries as well as overall results. Consider having a summary per constituency per source.

Step 4: The teams reconvene after sufficient time has been allocated for each person to complete the assignment. The purpose of this is to reconcile any differences that may be there and/or to see if there are any glaring omissions that should be included. Other things that might be discussed are clarity of entries that are to be placed into a final summary and whether they are brief and free of excess verbiage. Equilibrium between these two criteria is struck. Then the final summaries are produced.

In most assessments, perhaps three ways of obtaining data will be used, leading to approximately the same number of summaries with key findings reflected in them. They will contain much information but are much shorter than the original data reports.

Step 5: The facilitator of the needs assessment collects the summaries and distributes copies to the NAC for review and discussion. This should be done about a week before a full group meeting about what seems to be emerging from the data.

The NAC members should examine the summaries as a prelude to decisions in relation to the most pressing needs that are corroborated across the sources. Questions that would guide the discourse could include the following:

- Is there a clear set of needs that are consistent across the sources?
- Are the data really pointing in the same direction without any contradictory evidence?
- Are the qualitative and quantitative data in agreement so that the combination of results makes a stronger case for a need rather than a source by itself?
- Is there any contradictory evidence, and, if so, what and how strong is it?
- Are there unique aspects of data from a source that also should be included in the summary?
- Similarly, are there parts of the data that although not in tune with the above points are so interesting that they should be included in a final report for the organization? It is OK to incorporate such data into the final framework so long as they are appropriately labeled.

Step 6: Convene the NAC and engage in a lively interchange about the final results and what is to be recommended to the organizational decision makers. When completed generate a report to those individuals, keeping it focused on main recommendations, with the short summaries appended for questions or concerns that occur.

❖ SAMPLES OF SHORT SUMMARIES

In Exhibits 4.1 and 4.2, samples of summaries are given. They are intended to provide a sense of what might be included.

Exhibit 4.1   Information From Databases on Childhood Immunizations

Methods Summary

Statewide records from the past 10 years

Local health department records

Information collected from elementary school nurses

Information found in school records (primarily of a large urban local district)

Specialized health department report from 3 years ago

Main Findings

- Overall statewide immunization rate has fallen below 75% in the period under investigation.

- Statewide rates are different depending on socioeconomic status (SES).

- Local health department rates parallel those of the state level.

- Local rates depend on SES, and there are disparities associated with ethnicity.

- School records parallel what is seen in the other records, but the disparities are somewhat greater than would be expected from the larger databases.

- School nurses report they think the rates are changing and improving as public health personnel are getting information out to individuals who directly serve the health needs of children.

- They see the disparity arising from SES as a pertinent factor affecting the health of very young children.

Contradictory Findings

- While the nurses agree that the rates are too high, they suspect that the data-based information is dated and the number of immunizations is on an upward trend.

Other Pertinent Information

- Nurses commented (on the survey that accompanied the request for records and information) that certain types of public policies may be affecting negatively what is being observed in the state, and they suggested that a small number of survey questions were vague.

- Some nurses and public health personnel contacted during the database analysis were concerned about the accuracy of the statistics in the base and the manner in which they were collected.

- It was not possible to derive or infer causes of the problem from the obtained information, which may indicate a need for a different and subsequent collection of data.

- It may be necessary to go back and analyze the data to see if any trends are apparent, especially for the last few years (are the rates changing and, if so, how?).

Exhibit 4.2   Survey Data

Methods Summary

Different versions of the same survey were developed for teachers, administrators, and various groups of users of a federally funded educational information service.

A stratified random sample of schools in the United States were selected for participation in the needs assessment.

Random groups of users were sampled.

Results were compared across different types of respondents.

Some of the items were generated from a search of the literature.

Main Findings

The distribution of teachers and administrators in the sample compared quite well to that of the U.S. population.

- The rate of survey return was not high due to contacting potential respondents late in the school year.

- Rates of awareness of the service from the nationwide samples of teachers and administrators were quite low with the latter being higher but slightly so.

- Gaps were considerable when the responses of teachers and administrators were compared for the availability of key resources in the schools—teachers always perceived much greater discrepancies than did administrators.

- Mechanisms by which teachers gain information were more diverse than originally expected.

- There are clusters of teacher types—some appear to be more amenable to the use of the service whereas others are less attracted.

- There were sharp disparities between frequent users and those who had accessed the service one time.

- A host of other findings from the somewhat lengthy survey

Contradictory Findings

- There is not much evidence of whether the rate of service use is too low since there are few comparative studies of similar efforts (no real baseline exists or can be inferred).

- No data are available to explain why the views of teachers and administrators even in the same school buildings are so different.

Other Pertinent Information

- Some aspects of data should be studied in depth for ways to better publicize the service given the mechanisms by which teachers gain new information.

- Since the return rates were fairly low, it is desirable that other sources of data be obtained and examined in light of what was learned from the surveys.

- The qualitative companion study should be consulted in relation to the point made above.

- If administrators distribute information in schools, it is possible that there were problems within individual schools in regard to this process.

A couple of things need to be emphasized about the exhibits. First, in most situations the entries will usually be more numerous than what has been given in the exhibits particularly if the NAC has been diligent about its work. The data will be rich in information, and it is best to the extent feasible to capture the prominent ideas in short phrases or sentences. Second, in the "Other Pertinent Information" section of Exhibit 4.2, there is reference to another method employed in this assessment. A concern might be raised about whether the team compiling the summary drifted from its focus on the one source as it had been instructed to do. Could this possibly bias its summary?

Yes, group members drifted, but that might not be bad. They were attentive to great degree to the pertinent data. But at the same time they have been members of an NAC investigating the topic area for a period of time. It would almost be impossible for them to divorce themselves from the process solely to focus on one source. By that token, it's OK for some ideas (although limited as much as practical) to be suggested in the summary. It also points out that the NAC has become inculcated in what the process entails and the value of collecting data in multiple ways and from unique sources. The goal is to derive as much as possible from the single source while being objective about all the data accessible to the committee.

Collated Summary Across Sources

At this juncture in the needs assessment it is possible to generate a collated table from the individual summaries. Salient findings from each would be incorporated into the table with the need in the row and the source(s) in the column heading. For each need, the findings would be listed (per source) with a final column for commenting about the agreement and commonalities across the various sources. It would require impartiality from those compiling the table to ensure the commentary is as fair and accurate as possible. Subclassifications such as contradictory evidence and/or other relevant information could be additional rows or columns as appropriate. The one caveat is that the more that is included, the more complex the visual display becomes. Too much information may adversely affect decision making. A collated summary like this could lead to an overly detailed table that is hard to follow when considering what is perceived to be the best recommendations to make to the organization. Too many specifics may cloud the field.

Therefore, we suggest not including too much about methods in the summary in the table. It would vary for each specific study and what was at risk in the course of action proposed to the decision makers. It is imperative to keep the table as focused as is possible. The shell might look something like Table 4.4. The table is a natural outgrowth of the summaries previously described. How should it be developed?

Table 4.4 Table Shell for a Collated Summary for Needs Assessment Data From Multiple Sources

	Source 1	Source 2	Source n	Commentary
Need Area 1 Main Findings Contradictory Evidence				
Need Area 2 Main Findings Contradictory Evidence				
Need Area n				

One approach is to discuss the individual summaries with the NAC and, after agreement, assign the facilitator to complete a draft that is reviewed by the committee. This is reasonable since that individual has been coordinating the activities throughout the process and has the most assessment experience. Another valid approach is to ask several good writers in the group to accept responsibility for compiling the table.

In either case, it should be reviewed one final time by the entire group. The criticality of a collated table cannot be understated. It will be a primary mechanism for communicating with all levels of organizational personnel. The individual source sheets serve as backup documentation for the table. All tables and summaries should be dated, as should work drafts for inclusion in the permanent record of the effort and its audit trail.

In terms of reviewing the collated table, we recommend the NAC utilize the following guiding questions:

- Do we feel that the entries for a cell under a source are an adequate representation of what was learned from it?

- Are there enough of the specifics in each cell without going into so much detail as to overcomplicate the process of seeing how the data did or did not come together?

- Is the commentary sufficient in pulling together the trends in the data or lack thereof, and is it in a form that will help the deliberations of the staff and decision makers?

- Is it transparent as to how the commentary was derived, and is there any bias or slant in sections of the table?

- What contradictory evidence is there that might affect how the need is viewed or eventually prioritized?

- How strong is the latter information?

These questions are based on the shell in Table 4.4. As noted, other tables may have more rows, columns, or queries to fit the situation. We encourage you to be probing and challenging as in all likelihood your work will become public later, particularly for nonprofit and tax-subsidized entities. This is the point at which any problems or discrepancies in the data or sources should be resolved by the NAC prior to moving forward.

Before highlights of the chapter, it is important to recall that combining the data in Phase II is a prelude to prioritizing needs. The better this is done, the smoother the process of arriving at final priorities. Since most assessments use multiple methods and constituencies, pulling all the data together meaningfully assumes a major place in the assessment endeavor.

Highlights of the Chapter

1. Over the years the practice of needs assessment has evolved with most schol-ars and practitioners advocating and using multiple methods often across diverse constituencies. This is what is seen more and more in published liter-ature about the topic (see Book 3).

2. Such practice makes it incumbent for the needs assessor(s) and the NAC to seek convenient ways to pull together the mass of data and information that will inevitably result.

3. Three basic ways of doing so were described in the text—goal attainment scores (GAS), short summaries per source, and a collated summary across sources.

4. The advantages and disadvantages of each were discussed along with steps for implementing each one of them.

5. As noted in other places in the KIT, once the NAC comes to agreement about which approach should be used, it would be helpful to date final tables and so forth to document the work that has been done in all phases of needs assessment.

6. Summarizing/juxtaposing data and information from multiple methods and sources is especially valuable input for the next major activity in dealing with needs. The tie to prioritization and making recommendations to the organi-zation is apparent.

7. Lastly, remember tables should be adapted to fit the dimensions and style of organizations. They are not nor should they represent rigid structures to be adhered to in lockstep formation.

5

Prioritizing
Identified Needs

❖ INTRODUCTION

Prioritization is perhaps the most glossed-over procedure in needs assessment. Several factors account for this. Assessment is an involved process that may take a significant commitment of human and financial resources. During the process the organization (via the needs assessment committee, or NAC) is obtaining a clearer picture of needs, why they exist, and potential solutions. As the assessment unfolds, needs may appear obvious, and it is not necessary to prioritize them. In some circumstances this is true; both the quantitative and the qualitative data point to what the priorities should be. Moreover, from discussions the facilitator senses that there is no disagreement on what should be emphasized. When these conditions occur there is no reason to complicate things anymore; move forward. The dated materials from previous work may be all that is required to support the priorities that are chosen.

But this is not always the case, especially in large-scale studies of needs. In many circumstances numerous important needs have been found that cannot be attended to at one time. There are just not enough resources. Attempting to work with too many can divide loyalties, dilute the effort, and limit the outcomes within the organization. A direct, more narrowly focused endeavor is the best approach.

Because decisions about priorities require the allocation of resources and can seriously impact how the organization delivers its goods and services, they will be questioned and challenged. Serious concerns could be raised:

- On what basis did you opt for these priorities?

- What criteria did you use to select these needs and not others?

- What process did you use to arrive at your decisions?

- Was it unbiased and reasonable?

- What are your thoughts on the likelihood of resolving the problems represented by these needs?

- Was there a consensus in the NAC about the target areas?

- If there were disagreements, what was their nature?

- Did subgroups within the context have different views of priorities, and if so, how were final priorities selected in light of the disparities?

Without a defensible prioritization strategy, problems will arise. By following a structured procedure there is documentation for how the final list was derived. It is the rationale for the choices and serves as an audit trail showing what went into the NAC's choices. It not only is useful now but also will serve as valuable input when a subsequent needs assessment is carried out at a later date.

What are the issues that push us toward a strict, more demanding way of determining priorities? Here are a few guidelines.

- What consequences can we envision if the needs aren't rectified or reduced?

- If we project into the future, what might be the losses and gains to be realized by not thinking of such needs?

- What should be new ventures and avenues for the organization?

- What might be the counterfactual state if we elect not to deal with the need or set of needs?

- Will our market share or our public image suffer if we choose to forget about the need?

- How many individuals are affected, and from what groups do they come?

- When we think about causes of needs, are they under the control of the organization, or are they ones that the organization can have an influence on and change?

- What is the nature of the need, and what is its size (how big a discrepancy is there)?

- What are the political ramifications of attending to or ignoring the needs, and if they are ignored, will the organization be able to handle any resulting political pressure?

- In accord with the prior question are there public relations issues if we don't attend to certain concerns?

- Will it be possible to mount a base of meaningful (not coerced) support for working on the need in the organization?

- How feasible is it for us to deal with the underlying problem?

- If additional sources of funds will be required, do we have an idea of what is available in the organization as well as external sources that could be accessed?

- Do we have a good feel for how a new or innovative direction will be supported or not supported by the organization and various segments within it?

These are just a small sampling of what can come up while prioritizing. Indeed many of the ideas embedded in the questions appear in various strategies for prioritizing.

It behooves the NAC to discuss the criteria for choosing needs. Those found in existing approaches are adequate, but the NAC is encouraged to discuss what to use based on the context and nature of the needs in its particular circumstance. When choices have to be defended, the time allocated for this endeavor will be worthwhile. A frank and open exchange here is good for bringing values to the forefront.

With this brief background, what might be a general set of steps in prioritizing? The following steps will fit most contexts.

❖ STEPS IN PRIORITIZING

Step 1: Make sure that a formal prioritizing procedure is a desirable course to pursue

As implied above, the NAC should engage in a brief discussion as to whether a formal or some sort of informal procedure would be useful. The committee may feel that the needs as priorities are already there, a lot is known about them and their importance, and overall the NAC is comfortable with the process at this point. The sense may be that it would not be of any importance to drag this out any longer, so let's enter into action planning (Phase III of needs assessment).

The NAC might think about any difficulties that doing so would incur. Is it being too hasty! What might be the consequences if the wrong choice was made? Would we benefit from a more formal prioritization rather than just relying on our perceptions? Should we quantify our priorities? When the assessment is for a small group of individuals or the recreational needs of a retirement community or a small department in a university, not much in the way of prioritizing may be required. Just how important is the decision anyways? We should press forward!

On the other hand, there may be serious consequences to attending to some needs at the expense of others. The politics (favoring one group over another, diverting resources from one activity to a different one) may be severe without carefully deriving priorities. When the choice can lead to divisiveness and resentment, then it is wise to thoughtfully select a means for determining final priorities. This will make the process more transparent to concerned stakeholders and other parties.

The most appropriate group for such deliberations is the NAC. The understanding of its members in this regard should be high and based on strong knowledge of the needs and the organization.

Step 2: Determine criteria for prioritizing needs

This is the most difficult and tenuous step in prioritizing. What are the criteria we should use, and what governs picking these instead of others? Consider Example 5.1.

Example 5.1

What Automobiles to Build and What Criteria Should Guide the Choice?

It is well known that there are greater profit margins for fully equipped large minivans, SUVs, and similar cars as compared to smaller fuel-efficient ones. In the '80s and '90s and up to just a few years ago when gasoline was in ample supply and considerably cheaper than it currently is, it was an easy decision to stress the profit incentive over that of the longer-term view of increasing miles per gallon. A short-term criterion was used to guide a major industry whose importance to the economy of the United

States cannot be overstated (this issue became critical since the inception of this writing when congressional hearings were held toward the end of 2008 and early in 2009 in regard to a potential, major bailout of indigenous U.S. automobile manufacturers. Indeed the fate of a large part of the U.S. economy was linked to this one segment of domestic production).

At the same time, gasoline was much more expensive in Europe, and hence smaller, less "gas-guzzling" cars were the norm. This presented a naturally occurring point of comparison to see what might happen if another scenario was to materialize.

Some manufacturers took a different stance (employed a different criterion if you will) and began to think about options such as fuel cells and hybrids. With the recent and sharp rises in energy costs, more efficient cars with the appropriate technology, especially hybrids, began to sell well, and the losses of the domestic companies mounted. Other factors have contributed to the decline in the national automobile industry, but the profit focus as opposed to a longer-term one played a significant part in its plight. Going further, Brazil via a target of severely reducing dependence on imported sources of energy for cars (a "what should be") began a farsighted program to achieve that end. Over a long period the country drastically limited the amount of fuel it purchased by various strategies including converting local crops to ethanol. Now, in the United States, similar strategies are being promoted.

So this seems to be a good way to go, but it also illustrates the complexity of criteria. There could always be a downside to the choices that guide priorities. Producing ethanol has its own costs, and as the supply of corn and other sources is diverted to fuel production, there is less of it for livestock with the result that food is likely to be more expensive in the future.

As a final note, when gas prices drop sharply it is possible that resolve and commitment in the United States to the long-term need may wane. In the first book of the KIT this pertains to the concept of short- and long-term thinking and the importance of not just focusing on immediate concerns.

A variety of criteria can be applied to making choices among needs. Some are importance to the organization's future (in the near term vs. down the road), feasibility for resolution within the organization or agency's purview, feasibility in conjunction with working and/or collaborating with other groups, relationship to the image or public stance of the organization (whether it would somehow lose favor and not look good if it did not work on a particular need), increasing and/or maintaining market share, maximizing/improving the quality of services, maximizing some aspect of what the organization does as in profits or getting ahead of the curve, minimizing risks to the organization, and others.

Within any criterion there are subcategories that could be used for making decisions. A quick search of the literature should yield enough concepts to spark and energize the discourse of the NAC.

Step 3: Choose a method for prioritizing

With criteria in hand, how should they be used to determine priorities? A number of easy to complex options are available, some of which are summarized in Table 5.1. Generally as one proceeds down the rows, the methods are more complex to implement. While that is the case, do not jump to the assumption that the methods nearer the bottom are better than those at the top. Methods fit different situations, and they may also produce similar choices.

Table 5.1   Methods Often Used for Prioritizing Needs

Method	Basic Description	Advantages	Disadvantages
Group discussion	Based on what has been learned in the needs assessment process, the NAC uses a discussion to arrive at a consensus	Easy to do Flows out of previous work and understanding of needs data Fits many situations A quick way to see if there is general agreement in the NAC Relatively fast procedure	Not particularly explicit with regard to criteria for choices Discussions can be dominated by a few influential members Probably doesn't align with cases where needs are complex or consequences are great May be harder to justify priorities if they are questioned
Rank-ordering	If the list of needs is not long, NAC members rank-order usually in terms of perceived importance	Easy to do Works well for shorter lists of needs Many variations of rank-ordering procedures can be used (see Book 1 in the KIT) Relatively fast procedure May permit seeing if there are disagreeing subgroups in the NAC	Often done on the basis of one criterion (importance) Too simplistic for complex needs Usually subtle and different meanings ascribed by rankers to the one criterion With many needs (>15) the rankers may have to use the rule of three or first selecting a subset of needs and then rank-ordering the items in it

Method	Basic Description	Advantages	Disadvantages
Zero sum game structure	Reviewers are assigned points (perhaps 10) and allot them to needs as appropriate Often points or symbols for them (stars, colors) are done in a group setting for needs posted on walls	If done in a group setting with color- or otherwise-coded symbols, it is easy to see subgroup patterns and resolve differences May require a rule such as only so many points can be assigned to one need Novelty and fun dimension that can enliven groups	Despite the fun aspect the points are allotted based on one criterion (importance) May not deal well with complex types of needs Without rules sometimes members of a group will place an undue number of points on their favored need
Using two or more criteria (simple format)	The NAC or a similar group looks at each need in terms of criteria such as importance to the organization and feasibility of resolution	Moderately easy to implement Requires group members to consider more criteria Many criteria can be used Can be done with yes/no responses or Likert scales for the criteria	While a step beyond the techniques above it may not go far enough with regard to complex needs Importance and feasibility criteria probably have to be broken into subparts
Multiple criteria with a screening mechanism	Multiple criteria are identified and then rank-ordered Each potential need is looked at in terms of the most important criterion first, and the ones that pass through that screen are examined in regard to the other criteria (screens) in order of their importance	More complex process that forces deeper thinking on the part of NAC members Ordering of criteria appears to be a good idea; some criteria are just more important than others Would rapidly reduce the number of needs for consideration For some areas (health, education) may work well	May fractionate the decision-making process because criteria often should be considered jointly instead of in isolation to each other As with any procedure, when it becomes more complicated implementation may be more difficult Not commonly observed in the conduct of needs assessments

(Continued)

Table 5.1 (Continued)

Method	Basic Description	Advantages	Disadvantages
	Those that pass through all the screens would be thought of as priorities (essentially a sifting process)		
Importance and feasibility ratings (more complex)	While other approaches deal with importance and feasibility, Sork (1998) divided the two criteria into logical subcategories for use in selecting the highest-priority needs Each importance and feasibility subcriterion is rated on a 1–5 scale, which subsequently leads to summed group ratings for the two categories	Requires that the committee rate each needs candidate carefully Deeper thought about prioritizing needs Additional criteria can be brought in and rated in the same manner as suggested by Altschuld and Witkin (2000) Other ways of doing the ratings are possible For complex and sensitive situations, the procedure provides a solid base for establishing priorities	Most groups have not done ratings like these and are unfamiliar with them Some individuals find this to be complicated and tedious Can be laborious, especially if a large number of needs are to be sorted through and dwindled down
Same as previous category with risk assessment formally included	Internal and external risks of attending or not attending to needs are added to the process	Makes the risk factor explicit in the prioritization decision May be particularly necessary in some needs assessments such as in health and public health preparedness (natural disasters, epidemics, terrorist attacks, etc.)	Adds another level of complication to prioritization Slows down prioritization Some aspects of risk may be quite subjective in judgment

Method	Basic Description	Advantages	Disadvantages
Prioritization embedded in strategic planning	Technique is called Causal-Utility Decision Analysis, or CUDA (Leigh, 2000) An NAC or other similarly constituted body would be charged with completing a four-celled grid with one dimension consisting of assets/liabilities (strengths/weaknesses) and the other being internal/external locus Each cell in the resultant grid is subdivided into three columns—issues, estimated costs and value (utility), and control (causality)	Pushes the NAC to be very analytical in its thought processes Use of the four cells and the subcategories in them is an excellent mechanism for engaging a planning group in discussion If the group was moderately large it could be split into smaller groups, which would complete the worksheets independently (it would be of interest and importance to see if they had related or identical ideas) Clever and novel way of attacking prioritization	Somewhat more involved and complex than a number of other techniques and may tax the patience of the NAC As described by Leigh (2000) and others there may be a tendency to attribute failure more to external than internal sources Will most likely require two passes to do, the first being done by individuals and the second by groups in a collective fashion

Additionally the more sophisticated approaches are not necessarily better, especially at the start of the process. Needs assessment is carried out in an atmosphere of continuous learning about issues, problems, concerns, deficits, and so forth. Going to full-blown, in-depth procedures may be overkill in many assessments. Where there are a lot of needs to be considered, perhaps it would be best to do one of the easier methods first and then follow it with a more involved one for a smaller set of needs. Simple methods do not require much time to implement. What to do depends on local circumstances and conditions and the perceptions of the facilitator as to what might suit the particular context.

Another subtle concern cutting across the entries is that multiple constituencies could have different views on which needs should be emphasized. Subgroups with their diverse values and perspectives might come to different conclusions about priorities. In a subtle way Hamann, DeCasper, and Ewald (2002) and Schnackenberg, Luik, Nisan, and Servant (2001) built this likelihood into their work. Priorities were determined for groups independently and then compared. This is a good strategy and should be part of all prioritizing efforts. What is required is a way to reconcile divergent priorities when they arise. Several things come to mind:

- Convene the groups for a discussion of why viewpoints were disparate and see if the disparities can be resolved.

- Think about selecting a need that is of relatively high priority for the groups but not at the top for any one of them (a compromise position) so that every constituency feels it is getting something from the assessment (a win-win proposition).

- Take the priority needs for the groups and then perform causal or cost analyses to see what might really be feasible and then let feasibility become a major factor in prioritization (somewhat embedded in a number of the procedures in the table).

- Consider doing some sort of revoting procedure whereby groups prioritize needs but are not permitted to use their first choice in the revised process.

Do not automatically anticipate disagreements because in many cases they will not be there or are minor and do not entail a lot of effort to gain group alignment. But when sharp disagreements occur, there can be difficulty in arriving at a set of priorities suitable to all. The facilitator's skills and knowledge in helping derive priorities will be critical at this juncture.

Lastly, note that the table is an overview of some of the methods for determining the most important needs. Others can be found in the literature. Additionally NACs and their facilitators are encouraged to adapt methods to the specifics of each individual needs assessment.

Step 4: Prioritize

4.a. A Simple Approach

Let's assume that you have picked a method for prioritizing. Let's look more closely at several of the methods in the table.

One of the authors led a small statewide professional group for 2 years. Just prior to his leadership role, the executive committee of the group (think of this as an NAC) went through a strategic planning effort facilitated by an external consultant. From it quite a few issues or needs emerged that were to be dealt with at a later date. Over the next month or so the author helped the group cluster the ideas together so that there were four or five main themes with subcategories underneath them. From there the group proceeded to prioritize as described in Example 5.2.

Example 5.2

Having Some Fun While Prioritizing!

The group consisted of 12 individuals. Each person was given a different-colored marker to use in rating needs that were clustered into categories with about five to six needs in each one. They came from discussions, the previous 2-day strategic planning meeting, and the subsequent review of what resulted from those activities. The clusters were written on separate sheets of poster paper, which were taped up around the room. (Make sure that the sheets are backed by another blank sheet since colored pens can leave marks on walls.)

The idea was to have the committee members take 10 points or dollars to allot to the needs after carefully reviewing all of the clusters and needs within them. Rules for the allocation were not specified. They could use the sum of 10 in any way they chose in regard to what they saw as the priorities for the organization for the next 2 years. The choice should be based on what they thought would be critically important to be done to move the association ahead.

Observing the group in action was informative. Initially, there was some normal joking and quiet discussion followed by much more silence. Slowly group members began to walk around the room looking closely at the clusters and the needs within them. The atmosphere wasn't somber, but it was serious. The quiet demeanor indicated how carefully people were thinking about using the 10 points. The consequences of the ratings were obvious to them and probably would be like that for most groups going through a similar prioritizing process.

The group also seemed to enjoy having the opportunity to walk around and then go about making choices in a somewhat novel way compared to what they would ordinarily do. It appeared that they had some fun along with having to do deeper contemplation.

It took more time than originally perceived due to each person pondering his or her choices. The care in considering possibilities was obvious. By this means, final priorities were determined and achieved by the group's follow-up work during the next 2 years. There were other needs, but they were of lesser importance and attention was not diverted to them.

The example illustrates the value and intensity of priority setting. Hard decisions have to be made, and prioritization is where the rubber meets the road. With that said, the procedure could have been improved in several ways. First, it would have been worthwhile to have rank-ordered the different clusters and assigned some sort of weights to them. While this is more complex it would be useful in many assessments. Second, it is beneficial to have more than one criterion for making judgments. Although the process worked well, using feasibility and importance would have helped get clearer distinctions between the needs.

Third and where it did not work so well was that the group failed to take into consideration that when a few raters placed all of their points on one or two needs, their decisions skewed the results. Because they held strong feelings about several needs, they were not forced to look at the full set (and elements within each need) using the 10-point approach.

Via the color coding it was relatively easy to spot the skewing and initiate a discussion. Ideally it would have been better for preestablished ground rules to guide a more subtle type of rating. The color coding saved the day, but the problem could have been avoided with better instructions on how to proceed. The NAC and facilitator are encouraged to explore, adapt, and adopt options to come up with a way to do simple ratings.

4.b. Using Multiple Criteria—A Little More Complex

The needs you are dealing with are too involved for a simple procedure. It is desirable to have the NAC or other decision-making groups think about more aspects of them before making choices. Multiple criteria must be employed. Table 5.2 contains an overview of how this might be done.

Table 5.2 Using Multiple Criteria to Prioritize Needs

Need Candidate	Importance (Yes/No)	Feasibility (Yes/No)	Cost Factor (High/Low)	Risk (High/Low)
1				
2				
3				
n				

Notice that the scale used for rating each of the needs has been limited to only 2 points. Even though there are four criteria it would be a fairly straightforward process for the committee members to quickly assign their individual perceptions to each need and then to collate them to see if there is agreement across the group. Thus it is possible to use numerous criteria for arriving at priorities without overcomplicating the process. Observe that several of the criteria seem to be about implementing solutions before priorities have been firmly established. Separating prioritization from action planning may be a little artificial, and it is not too surprising to see cost as a column heading.

Prioritization is dependent on well-thought-out and explicit criteria. Without such, the process is messier, and following that vein of thinking Example 5.2 would have been improved if the rating group had been supplied with better definitions upon which to base its choices.

What might happen if we went further in regard to more depth for prioritization? Sork (1998) divided importance and feasibility categories into five and three subareas, respectively. Each was rated on a 5-point scale. Altschuld and Witkin (2000) added risk to the equation and divided it into internal and external categories with subcategories within them. Beyond this there are other possibilities such as motivation to resolve a need or whether the need will become more severe or lessen with the passage of time. Criteria are important as is the level of detail built into them. Having subcategories and using scaling may be appealing, but these actions come with the cost of adding complexity to the work of the committee. How should the NAC proceed?

The answer depends on the needs being examined and the characteristics of the decision-making milieu. Our suggestion would be to stay as simple as possible unless it seems that doing so may not work. Or sophistication might only be needed for several criteria with others being left at a simple dichotomous response level.

Many options are there; choose what would be best for the local context and what would resonate with audiences for the needs assessment. Table 5.2 is a generic template to guide prioritization. One other point remains for our discussion.

4.c. Linking Prioritization to Strategic Planning

Throughout the process of assessing needs we are focusing attention on a smaller and smaller set of discrepancies. There is a continuous review and interchange going on regarding identification of needs and exploration of their causes and solutions. So the concept of interweaving strategic planning, needs assessment, and prioritization makes good sense. Here is how it might be done.

In Figure 5.1, a grid is provided that consists of four cells similar to the strengths, weaknesses, opportunities, and threats (SWOTs) commonly seen in strategic planning. The one difference is the division of the locus of control into whether it is internal to the organization or external to it. In Figure 5.2, there is a brief look into one of the cells in Figure 5.1.

Figure 5.1   General Strategic Planning Grid

	Assets	Liabilities
Internal	(Strengths)	(Weaknesses)
External	(Opportunities)	(Threats)

Figure 5.2   Expansion of the First Cell in the General Grid

Assets (Strength—Internal)	
Estimated Cost/Value (Utility)	Control

The grid helps in selecting areas of emphasis, and it might be best to complete cells for each of five or six seemingly important needs that require attention. This is a reasonable course of action if the number is not enormously high and if there is a strong feeling that looking at needs this way would be appropriate. Then taking the assets internal cell as a case in point, the NAC would examine issues pertinent to that cell, the costs and utility of the assets available, and what factors related to them are under control of the organization. This is a simplified version of what was proposed by Leigh (2000).

What are the resources associated with the asset? What might be the utility of using them—what values (consequences) might be enhanced by employing or accessing a resource (or resources)? What parts or how much of it is under the control of the organization? (Control deals with causal factors in terms of the need.) From that first cell, all other cells in the table would similarly be analyzed for each area of need.

Once tables are completed for the six needs, the NAC compares them to see the most likely candidates to pursue. Leigh (2000) briefly suggested how the categories of costs and control could be scaled or more highly quantified. Which need really has more internal assets that are under the aegis or management of the organization? What need areas would have the most potential opportunities, and what would be causal issues for those opportunities? From this analysis the NAC would select the main focus for the organization.

SWOTs, costs, values, and causal ideas are major inputs for developing action steps for the organization. While most of the other entries in Table 5.1 are more often used in needs assessment, linking strategic planning or some adaptation of it for prioritization purposes would be another course of action available to the NAC.

Highlights of the Chapter

1. Stress was put on the fact that procedures for prioritization are often neglected. Reasons for this were given.

2. Formal prioritization may not be too necessary in a variety of needs assessment situations. When the consequences of actions have major impact, then formal and defensible ways of establishing priorities are recommended.

3. Some preliminary questions for the NAC to consider were offered.

4. A number of basic to more complex techniques were overviewed in regard to their structure, strengths, and weaknesses.

5. In many instances there will be different constituencies participating in an assessment that, in turn, could arrive at quite distinct priorities. When this happens the process becomes more difficult. A few ways of dealing with this type of event were provided.

6. Several examples of determining priorities were described to provide some insight into the prioritization process.

7. Emphasis was placed on tailoring prioritization to the specific contours and special features of local circumstances.

8. It is useful to consult the literature to see how others went about the process of coming up with their needs emphases. What did they do? What can be learned from their effort that fits your situation? What could be improved or changed in their strategy? Are there things that should be avoided?

6

Some Nagging Afterthoughts and Caveats

❖ WHY THIS CHAPTER?

This chapter is included because of a problem that has been alluded to throughout the book. It is hidden and remains just beneath the surface. We want you to join us in thinking about it and in improving the science and art of needs assessment.

Most assessments (the processes involved and the results) are not published or presented in a manner available to other needs assessors and the research community interested in the topic. While practitioners may not be heavily invested in research, it is through research and publication that we inform others. What is learned from practice is invaluable, and often discussion about the conduct of assessments is not found in the literature. As concerns are encountered and addressed we encourage you to share them with the field by turning them into journal articles or reports accessible to an audience larger than an internal organizational one.

How were snags dealt with? Are there some quick and cheap ways of collecting data that may work as well as the more expensive ones? What trade-offs could be made with regard to the quality of instruments and measures that are based on the discrepancy definition of need? How are needs assessment data used in the organization? What changes were made in policies and operations based on the results of explorations of needs? How well did they work? How were political issues addressed and resolved? What would needs assessment committees (NACs) and their facilitators do differently the next time they engage in an assessment? We are all travelers on this journey, and guidance and insight are sought and always welcome.

❖ PROBLEMS IN NEEDS ASSESSMENT DATA AND SOURCES

Brief summaries of problems in needs assessment are provided in Tables 6.1 and 6.2. The entries give a flavor of some of the difficulties. In the tables, an issue for one type of method might also fit another.

Table 6.1 Some Problems in Qualitative Data Sources*

Method	Typical Problem(s)	Commentary
Focus Group Interviews (FGIs)	Replication Sampling Group leadership Interpretation of results Overinterpretation of results especially if replication does not occur	Obviously there are a number of ways that the technique could go astray and if not attended to could lead to less useful needs assessment data
Community Group Forums	Incomplete attendance or absence of some groups Inadequate planning for what seems on the surface to be a fairly easy-to-use technique Avoiding dominance by some in the group Maintaining focus Group leadership	It is wise to replicate forums, but costs dramatically will rise as will the planning efforts required Logistical concerns should not be minimized
Interviews	Training of interviewers Consistency of interviews Time to conduct Fatigue of interviewers if too many interviews are done per day	Technique is dependent on interviewers following protocols while at the same time sensing when to probe Guard against interviewers subtly cueing responses

Method	Typical Problem(s)	Commentary
Nominal Group Technique (NGT)	Replication Not following the rules may lead to a discussion group, not a NGT Limits to the kind of information produced	Like a FGI this is a small-group technique so replication is important Need to understand what the technique is supposed to do and what the main information produced is like
Observations	Sampling of situations and/or people to observe Interpretation of results Skills and training of the observer	See the above entries for similar problems that also fit observations

*Keep in mind that most qualitative techniques do not produce or lead directly to discrepancies; needs have to be inferred. Hence the need for multimethod approaches should be apparent.

Table 6.2   Summary of Some Problems in Quantitative Data and Data Sources*

Method	Sampling of Problem(s)	Commentary
Surveys	Incomplete item responses Return rates Not often double scaled Rationale for subtracting one score from another Wording problems "What should be" questions might reflect wants Prestructuring of the questionnaire may lead to "what should be" items that are of uniform high importance creating a skewed distribution Prestructuring may lead to issues with discrepancy scores	There is a host of difficulties that affect analysis and interpretation of survey data Many needs assessment surveys are not designed in accord with definition of need with only one dimension measured

Table 6.2 (Continued)

Method	Sampling of Problem(s)	Commentary
Data From Databases	How did the data get into the base? How does what was entered relate to interpretation? Missing data (incomplete files) may reflect subtle self-selection Qualitative data with numeric database information are very useful but may not be in the database Limited to what data are included in the base (whether they do or do not align with the needs under investigation)	Religious adherence to databases without understanding how factors such as those in the previous column affect interpretation It may be wise to either observe or track down how entries to the base are made How often is the base updated
Research and Other Quantitative Sources	Additional information is always useful in needs assessment work but avoid against overgeneralization Are the sources (research literature, prior evaluations, etc.) in agreement, or is there at least no contradictory evidence regarding needs?	Look closely at the samples used in prior efforts for purposes of comparison and generalizing

*For another interesting set of problems occurring in quantitative data and especially in calculating discrepancies, see Lee, Altschuld, and White (2007b).

Along the lines of the two tables, Altschuld and Witkin (2000) identified a set of difficulties encountered in methods and data and ones that occur during the process. They perceived that there were four generic categories in which assessments might go off the mark:

1. Determining estimates of current status:
   - Many variables (drug abuse, tobacco use, alcoholism, etc.) are not easily measured.

- Data may not be reliable and/or valid especially if they come from self-reports.
- Information derived from multiple sources may not agree.
- Data in existing sources either may be dated or may not be able to capture fast-moving trends.

2. Determining "what should be" status:

- In many areas (wellness, physical activity) standards for what should be are lacking or not fully agreed upon.
- It may be difficult to decide on standards in education, wellness, recreation, and other related fields.
- "What should be's" may represent wants as opposed to realistic endpoints.
- Consistently high ratings of what should be may be obtained, particularly where the needs assessor and NAC have done extensive literature review and other work prior to the development of the survey (i.e., careful preselection of categories and items for the instrument).
- Categories on assessment surveys may not be rank-ordered in terms of their importance to the area in consideration.

3. Determining discrepancies:

- Discrepancies are for wants instead of meaningful "what should be" conditions (getting rid of wants is sometimes hard to do).
- What is the size of a discrepancy or gap that warrants attention (is a large gap for a small group more important than a lesser gap for a larger group)?
- The task of dealing with multiple sources of data when trying to arrive at a discrepancy is challenging.
- Qualitative data are not amenable to discrepancy analysis, and therefore inferences about discrepancies have to be made.

4. Determining needs in general:

- The use of multiple methods in needs assessment although encouraged greatly complicates the process, and amalgamating data from multiple constituencies and sources can be complex.
- Obtaining agreement about priority needs across distinct, involved groups of stakeholders can be daunting.
- Undue reliance may be placed on one source that often is quantitative in nature.

To these entries many more issues could have been added. What about short- and long-term thinking? Some methods are costly, so what shortcuts and trade-offs might be used? What are the best reporting formats or, even better, what formats should be employed for various constituency groups? What do we know and understand about the nature of instruments incorporated into assessments? What are good mechanisms for communicating in the organization, and what would be the most appropriate times to do so? The list goes on and on!

Beyond that, the assessment must deal with getting results implemented, communicating outcomes outside of the organization, ensuring involvement of the key individuals, and so forth (Altschuld, 2004). Depending on the size of the organization and the types of needs being dealt with, the whole enterprise can become quite complex.

❖ IN LIGHT OF THESE PROBLEMS, WHAT CAN THE NEEDS ASSESSOR DO?

One obvious answer is to simply forego the venture. There are too many obstacles, some that seem insurmountable. At times that might be an option, but for the most part we don't really consider it viable. That wasn't the intent in highlighting the problems, but rather it was to advocate a more contemplative stance. Despite all the issues, needs are important for organizations and are the basis for many actions (Hansen, 1991). Needs will frequently outweigh existing resources, but hard decisions about priorities still have to be made. It is better in our judgment to formally assess needs than not to. An imperative therefore is that the NAC and facilitator have an overall schema for assessment and needs-based decision making and that it is tempered with an understanding of the subtleties in the process.

So thinking about the list of problems, first, like all applied social science methods, those used in needs assessment have pros and cons, advantages and disadvantages, with some of the negatives being hard to fix. There will be compromises made in practical applications of methods and inadequacies in sampling, quality of instruments, and the nature and utility of the information generated. Second, recognize that by using multiple methods, the strength of corroboration via different techniques can frequently offset weaknesses in one source and enhance the arguments in favor of a set of needs. In a probabilistic sense, the odds against three or four sets of results all pointing toward the same need would be unlikely, and if that was observed, weaknesses in any one or several methods would be compensated for and minimized. When the evidence agrees, it can be powerful and persuasive.

Third, there are numerous ways to conduct an assessment that are helpful in ameliorating the difficulties encountered in the process. Consider the results of a survey that may be difficult to interpret. Would it not be useful to initiate a focus group where knowledgeable community participants receive the results in advance along with some general questions to guide their thinking about meaning and interpretation? Group or individual interviews are excellent opportunities to probe what the results are saying and why interviewees perceive them in certain ways.

Or why not do a focus group interview before designing the instrument? If a focus group is not possible, field testing with a small group and debriefing afterward would work well. What items were not clear, or were some choices missing? Were the directions clear? How would participants' peers respond to the instrument? Should other questions be asked? On the face of it (face validity), do the questions make sense? Doing these types of activities greatly enhanced the quality of the survey used by White, Altschuld, and Lee (2006b) and led to numerous changes in parts of a double-scaled one developed by Manchester (2007). Interestingly in the latter case the debriefing was done via e-mail since the small group was dispersed across a state.

In the same regard, while reviewing the literature is a *sine qua non* (necessary) condition for gaining insight into content and potential structure of survey items, it will often be insufficient. It probably will not provide enough detail into such things as how people refer to a term in common vernacular, the intensity of their feelings and perceptions, or the subtle nature of body language while discussing a topic. Focus groups and individual interviews bring these nuances to the surface and improve the instruments employed in a needs assessment.

Another way to deal with problems is akin to the peer review procedure coming from qualitative research (Patton, 2001). When assessment results are seemingly hard to understand (and this situation occurs more than we would like to admit), convene a small panel of experts from nearby universities or agencies or specialists in needs assessment to review what has been produced. Provide them with a list of questions/concerns prior to meeting as a mechanism for focusing their thoughts. Examples of what might be looked at include

- the quality of the questions used in the investigation;

- the adequacy of the sampling frames and the actual samples realized (was it a cross section of concerned parties and stakeholders, and was the sample size sufficient?);

- the degree to which there is compelling (strong) evidence for specific needs that could be recommended to a decision-making body;

- the validity of the conclusions that have been drawn by the NAC;

- the overall quality of the implementation of all parts of the process (Phases I and II and III if applicable);

- areas of weakness in implementation;

- needs for which more information would be desirable;

- glaring omissions in what was looked at; and

- related concerns.

This is in essence a kind of meta-evaluation of what the NAC has done during the assessment and the meaningfulness of the outcomes achieved.

After each panelist has examined what has been done, convene a meeting for serious discussion of queries such as those above or others panelists sense should be addressed. Look for agreements and dis-agreements. This is an excellent way to get feedback and learn from colleagues. The time spent and the expenditure of funds (remuneration for the panelists) on this activity are a wise use of resources.

A version of this procedure was done for the minority student retention project mentioned previously. It had a steering committee composed of mostly minority faculty members and administrators in science, technology, engineering, and mathematics fields from 15 uni-versities. About once a year a detailed summary of evaluation results (many from double- and triple-scaled survey items) was presented to the group, and a series of interpretive questions was put to the collec-tive body. The evaluators simply became analogous to needs assess-ment facilitators in leading the session. The discussion was intense with many possible interpretations discussed as well as new directions for the project. One caveat was that the concern and thinking generated by the data were so strong that other business of the committee could not be conducted. Perhaps it would have been better to have focused the exchange on only several key concerns.

When reporting to decision makers, incorporate what has been learned from the peer review or sources such as just described. For a peer review, explain how the panel was selected, the use of the advance organizer questions, the main perceptions of the reviewers, and so on. Their input and involvement should increase the validity of the assessment and what is being proposed for action steps.

Throughout the KIT, the importance of creatively combining methods in needs assessment has been stressed. That is because the way to proceed with an assessment is not always obvious when the endeavor starts; rather it tends to emerge as the process unfolds. You cannot always anticipate or know what will be needed for an assessment. Budgetary flexibility is essential when the data are complex or the results are in conflict. That is precisely when it may become necessary to secure outside expertise. It is helpful to have the ability to apply funds in unique ways as activities are being conducted and to convince the NAC and administration why contingency plans for unforeseen circumstances are important. It is the safety net of the needs assessment. By the same token, if the data are straightforward, do not use these resources just because they are there. You may learn enough in Phase I or through some simple and inexpensive Phase II methods so that the extra funds do not have to be spent.

❖   REITERATING THAT CRITICAL
PUBLISHING ROLE FOR NEEDS ASSESSORS

Needs assessments generally fall into patterns that should be fairly easy to classify. But from the same vantage point, every one of them has its unique aspects and features. There may be combinations of methods that work in one situation but not another. Why they worked in one circumstance and not others is critical information for understanding how to improve practice. Some needs assessors may see specialized ways to analyze and report the results such as in the goal attainment table described in Chapter 4 (Table 4.2). Others may find better ways to convey survey data that are utilitarian for decision making or to explain obstacles in doing an assessment and how they were overcome.

Needs assessments can be expensive. Some may find cost-effective ways of locating and collecting data or an unusually good source (or sources) of existing information for a topic area as in vocational rehabilitation or, better yet, find strategies that expedite the entire process. Ways to be more effective and efficient are valuable information for all involved in conducting these types of activities.

Most of this is lost to the field because it is not published or reports aren't widely circulated. (This was a bit of a problem in locating information for the first four books in the KIT and for the prior two by Altschuld and Witkin [2000] and Witkin and Altschuld [1995].) Thus the field grows more slowly than it should. This is easy for us to espouse since we are academics and would push the need for publications—it is part of our professional reward structure. Why should this be important to the practitioner?

By analogy, in academic medicine, research and publication are necessary to maintain the institution's standing in higher education and continued support (funding) for future studies. And most assuredly we look to researchers for the cutting-edge breakthroughs that enhance and prolong our lives. The motto is "publish or perish." Without such research one of the authors would be literally blind and more than likely suffering from heart disease.

By the same token there are numerous medical practitioners who have little to gain by getting into the literature, yet they do so when they note some unusual occurrence in their practice. The rapid rise of HIV/AIDS was brought to the forefront by such individuals and undoubtedly shortened the time it took to recognize the seriousness of the epidemic and seek ways to treat and stem its spread. Clinical research has significance, and findings from it have certainly led to more controlled studies.

Similarly needs assessment practitioners should report what they are doing to a wide audience, and going further they might actually conduct research studies embedded in the context of their assessments. For example, funds could be divided across different qualitative techniques to see if they produce the same kind of information. With regard to quantitative methods and surveys specifically, if they are complex and the samples are large, why not use two or three versions of an instrument with a common section and then random item samples for others? If the common sections yielded equivalent results, the views of the overall sample on the other sections could then be inferred and estimated from the smaller samples. This would yield very useful information and at the same time reduce the burden placed on the majority of respondents.

In terms of another research idea practitioners might opt to explore synthetic estimation (using social indicators in formulas to predict certain types of mental health or health needs) to see how well it works in local situations. Were the predictions accurate and, even more important, useful for making decisions? Could different indicators have been incorporated into the formulas to improve the quality of results? What are they, and why did they enhance the effort? This is the type of valuable knowledge that we propose should be gained from needs assessments carried out in field settings.

Has the practice of needs assessment been evaluated in relation to instances where it has been less than successful? Do we know what factors promote the success of an assessment and those that inhibit it especially for the utilization of outcomes? What about evaluations of how studies were implemented and how an NAC established the focus and direction? How well does the three-phase model underlying the Needs Assessment KIT work—does it make sense in the real world? Are there assessments that have been carried out on a cyclical basis and that have databases and other types of regularly kept information? Have benchmarks been established and then employed to help an organization maintain or improve its mission and services? What kinds of organizational barriers and blinders regarding needs assessment have arisen? How were they overcome—what mechanisms were helpful? How was support gained from the top level of the institution, agency, or business? What communication strategies worked best and why? It is obvious that the list of possibilities in terms of practitioner-driven studies is large.

There is as much of a major role for practitioners in guiding what we do in the field of needs assessment as there is for academics. We know there is more tacit knowledge about the process than appears in the formal literature, and it would have major import for improving how to go about assessing needs.

Won't you join us in providing it?

References

Altschuld, J. W. (2004). Emerging dimensions of needs assessment. *Performance Improvement, 43*(1), 10–15.

Altschuld, J. W., Anderson, R., Cochrane, P., Frechtling, J., Frye, S., & Gansneder, B. (1997). *Evaluation of the Eisenhower national clearinghouse for mathematics and science education.* Columbus: The Ohio State University.

Altschuld, J. W., Kumar, D. D., Smith, D. W., & Goodway, J. D. (1999). School-based educational innovations: Case illustrations of context-sensitive evaluations. *Journal of Family & Community Health, 22*(1), 66–79.

Altschuld, J. W., & Witkin, B. R. (2000). *From needs assessment to action: Transforming needs into solution strategies.* Thousand Oaks, CA: Sage.

Anderson, C. L., Jesswein, W. A., & Fleischman, W. (1990). Needs assessment based on household and key informant surveys. *Evaluation Review, 14*(2), 182–191.

Anderson, T., & Kanuka, H. (2003). *E-research: Methods, strategies, and issues.* Upper Saddle River, NJ: Allyn & Bacon.

Applied Survey Research. (1999). *1999 Monterey County homeless census and needs assessment.* Watsonville, CA: Author.

Applied Survey Research. (2002). *Homeless census and homeless youth/foster teen study: Monterey County 2002.* Watsonville, CA: Author.

Archer, T. (2003). Web-based surveys. *Journal of Extension, 41*(4). Retrieved February 9, 2006, from http://www.joe.org/joe/2003august/tt6.shtml

Braun, K., Hammond, O., & Kana'iaupuni, S. (2006, September). *What's happening in Hawaii-Pacific evaluation?* Panel presentation to the annual meeting of the Hawaii-Pacific Evaluation Association, Waikiki, HI.

Bunch, M. B. (1980). *Nutrition education needs assessment final report: 1980.* Durham, NC: NTS Research Corporation.

Bunch, M. B., & Watson, D. J. R. (1986). *Maryland nutrition education needs assessment, final report and supplements.* College Park, MD: State Department of Education.

Centers for Public Health Preparedness Network of Evaluators. (2006). *Lessons learned regarding education evaluation methods in the centers for public health preparedness network: A promising practices resource database.* Washington, DC: Association of Schools of Public Health.

Chambers, R. L. (2005). *Imputation verses estimation of finite population distributions* (Southampton Statistical Sciences Research Institute Monograph No. M05/06). Highfield, Southampton, United Kingdom: University of Southampton.

Chatelle, M., & Tornquist, K. K. (2007, August). *Greater Longview United Way 2007 needs assessment*. Retrieved December 15, 2008, from http://www.longviewunitedway.org/media/2007CNA.pdf

Chauvin, S. W., Anderson, A. C., & Bowdish, B. E. (2001). Assessing the professional development needs of public health professionals. *Journal of Public Health Management and Practice, 7*(4), 23–27.

Clem, C. (2003, May). *Results of data analysis: NIC needs assessment on correctional management and executive leadership development.* Washington, DC: U.S. Department of Justice.

Community Research Partners. (2005). *Community indicators database report: A picture of trends and conditions in central Ohio.* Retrieved February 3, 2009, from http://www.communityresearchpartners.org/uploads/publications//CommunityIndicatorsdb_v3.1.pdf

Cronbach, L. J. (1951). Coefficient alpha and the internal structure of tests. *Psychometrika, 16,* 297–334.

Dell, D. L. (1974, April). *Magnitude estimation scaling in needs assessment.* Paper presented at the annual meeting of the American Educational Research Association, Chicago.

Demarest, L., Holey, L., & Leatherman, S. (1984, October). *The use of multiple methods to assess continuing education needs.* Paper presented at the joint meeting of the Evaluation Network and Evaluation Research Society, San Francisco.

DeMille, N. (2004). *Night fall.* New York: Hachette Book Group.

DeVellis, R. F. (2003). *Applied Social Research Method Series: Vol. 36. Scale development: Theory and application* (2nd ed.). Thousand Oaks, CA: Sage.

DiLalla, D. L., & Dollinger, S. J. (2006). Cleaning up data and running preliminary analysis. In F. T. L. Long & J. T. Austin (Eds.), *The psychology research handbook: A guide for graduate students and research assistants* (2nd ed., pp. 241–253). Thousand Oaks, CA: Sage.

Dillman, D. A. (2000). *Mail and Internet surveys: The tailored design method.* New York: John Wiley & Sons, Inc.

Dillman, D. A. (2004). Internet surveys: Back to the future. *The Evaluation Exchange, 3,* 6–7.

Fiorentine, R. (1993). Beyond equity in the delivery of alcohol and drug abuse treatment services. *Journal of Drug Issues, 23*(4), 559–577.

Fiorentine, R. (1999). After drug treatment: Are 12-step programs effective in maintaining abstinence? *American Journal of Drug and Alcohol Abuse, 25*(1), 93–116.

Furr, R. M., & Bacharach, V. R. (2008). *Psychometrics: An introduction.* Thousand Oaks, CA: Sage.

Guercio, M. (2001). Principles, methods, and instruments for the creation, preservation and use of archival records in the digital environment. *American Archivist, 64*(2), 238–269.

Gunn, H. (2002). *Web-based surveys: Changing the survey process.* First Monday. Retrieved August 13, 2009, at http://firstmonday.org/htbin/cgiwrap/bin/ojs/index.php/fm/article/view/1014

Hamann, M. S. (1997). *The effects of instrument design and respondent characteristics on perceived needs.* Unpublished doctoral dissertation, The Ohio State University, Columbus.

Hamann, M. S., DeCasper, H., & Ewald, K. (2002). *Using formal needs assessment data in ongoing strategic planning.* Paper presented to the annual meeting of the American Evaluation Association, Baltimore.

Hansen, D. J. (1991). *An empirical study of the structure of needs assessment.* Unpublished doctoral dissertation, The Ohio State University, Columbus.

Hershkowitz, M. (1974). *Statewide educational needs assessment: Results from selected model states.* Silver Spring, MD: Hershkowitz Associates.

Hopkins, K. D. (1998). *Educational and psychological measurement and evaluation* (8th ed.). Needham Heights, MA: Allyn & Bacon.

Hung, H.-L., Altschuld, J. W., & Lee, Y.-F. (2008). Methodological and conceptual issues confronting a cross-country Delphi study of educational programs. *Evaluation and Program Planning, 31*(2), 191–198.

Kaufman, J. S., & Cooper, R. S. (1999). Seeking causal explanations in social epidemiology. *American Journal of Epidemiology, 150*(2), 113–120.

Kaufman, R. (1983). Needs assessment. In F. W. English (Ed.), *Fundamental curriculum decisions* (pp. 53–67). Alexandria, VA: Association for Supervisory and Curriculum Development.

Kosecoff, J., & Fink, A. (1982). *Evaluation basics: A practitioner's manual.* Beverly Hills, CA: Sage.

Kumar, D. D., & Altschuld, J. W. (1999). Evaluation of interactive media in science education: A contextual approach. *Journal of Science Education and Technology, 8*(1), 55–65.

Lee, Y.-F., Altschuld, J. W., & White, J. L. (2007a). Effects of multiple stakeholders in identifying and interpreting perceived needs. *Evaluation and Program Planning, 30*(1), 1–9.

Lee, Y.-F., Altschuld, J. W., & White, J. L. (2007b). Problems in needs assessment data: Discrepancy analysis. *Evaluation and Program Planning, 30*(3), 258–266.

Leigh, D. (2000). Causal-utility decision analysis (CUDA): Qualifying SWOTs. In E. Biech (Ed.), *The 2000 Annual: Vol. 2. Consulting* (pp. 261–265). San Francisco, CA: Jossey-Bass/Pfeiffer.

Manchester, J. (2007). *Factors influencing evaluation scope of coalitions on formative to summative levels.* PhD dissertation, The Ohio State University, United States. Retrieved February 20, 2009, from ProQuest Digital Dissertations database (Publication No. AAT 3260171).

Mertler, C. A., & Vanatta, R. A. (2005). *Advanced and multivariate statistical methods: Practical applications and interpretation* (3rd ed.). Glendale, CA: Pyrczak.

Meyers, L. S., Gamst, G., & Guarino, A. J. (2006). *Applied multivariate research: Design and interpretation.* Thousand Oaks, CA: Sage.

Moore, D. M. (2006). *The basic practice of statistics* (4th ed.). New York: W. H. Freeman & Co.

Mosely, J. L., & Heaney, M. J. (1994). Needs assessment across disciplines. *Performance Improvement Quarterly, 7*(1), 60–79.

Passmore, D. L. (1990). Epidemiological analysis as a method of identifying safety training needs. *Human Resource Development Quarterly, 1,* 277–293.

Patten, M. L. (2009). *Understanding research methods: An overview of the essentials* (7th ed.). Glendale, CA: Pyrczak.

Patton, M. Q. (2001). *Qualitative research and evaluation methods* (3rd ed.). Thousand Oaks, CA: Sage.

Pedhazur, E. J. (1997). *Multiple regression in behavioral research: Explanation and prediction* (3rd ed.). Fort Worth, TX: Harcourt Brace College Publishers.

Reid, L. (2005, August). *Keynote address to the Ohio Science and Engineering Alliance Summer Research Forum.* University of Akron, Akron, OH.

Salkind, N. J. (2006). *Tests and measurement for people who think they hate tests and measurement.* Thousand Oaks, CA: Sage.

Sampson, R. J., Laub, J. H., & Wimer, C. (2006). Does marriage reduce crime? A counterfactual approach to within-individual causal effects. *Criminology, 44*(3), 465–508.

Satcher, D., Kosecoff, J., & Fink, A. (1980). Results of a needs assessment strategy in developing a family practice program in an inner-city community. *Journal of Family Practice, 10,* 871–879.

Schnackenberg, H. L., Luik, K. L., Nisan, Y., & Servant, C. (2001). A case study of needs assessment in teacher in-service development. *Educational Research and Development, 7*(2–3), 137–160.

Shannon, D. M., Johnson, T. E., Searcy, S., & Lott, A. (2002). Using electronic surveys: Advice from survey professionals. *Practical Assessment, Research & Evaluation, 8*(1). Retrieved December 15, 2008, from http://pareonline.net/getvn.asp?v=8&n=1

Sork, T. J. (1998). Program priorities, purposes, and objectives. In P. S. Cookson (Ed.), *Program planning for the training and continuing education of adults: North American perspectives* (pp. 273–300). Malabar, FL: Krieger.

Stacey, A. G. (2005). The reliability and validity of the item means and standard deviations of ordinal level response data. *Management Dynamics.* Retrieved December 12, 2008, from http://findarticles.com/p/articles/mi_qa5465/is_200507/ai_n21386649

Stanton, J. S., & Rogelberg, S. G. (2001). Using Internet/Intranet Web pages to collect organizational data. *Organizational Research Methods, 4,* 199–216.

Stevens, J. P. (2007). *Intermediate statistics: A modern approach* (3rd ed.). New York: Lawrence Erlbaum Associates.

Stockdill, S., & Kraus, L. (2009). *Developing a model comprehensive statewide needs assessment with corresponding training materials for state VR agency staff and SRC members* (provisional document). Berkeley, CA: InfoUse.

Tabachnik, B. G., & Fidell, L. S. (2006). *Using multivariate statistics* (5th ed.). New York: Harper & Row.

Trochim, W., & Donnelly, J. P. (2007). *The research methods knowledge base* (3rd ed.). Cincinnati, OH: Atomic Dog Publishing.

Warner, R. M. (2008). *Applied statistics: From bivariate through multivariate techniques.* Thousand Oaks, CA: Sage.

Watson, D. J. R., & Bunch, M. B. (1983, July). *Statewide needs assessment: A multi-methodological approach.* Paper presented to Society for Nutrition Education, Denver, CO.

White, J. L., Altschuld, J. W., & Lee, Y.-F. (2006a). Cultural dimensions in science, technology, engineering and mathematics. *Journal of Educational Research and Policy Studies, 6*(2), 41–59.

White, J. L., Altschuld, J. W., & Lee, Y.-F. (2006b). Persistence of interest in science, technology, engineering, and mathematics: A minority retention study. *Journal of Women and Minorities in Science and Engineering, 12*(1), 47–64.

Williams, H., Harris, R., & Turner-Stokes, L. (2007). Northwick Park Care needs assessment: Adaptation for inpatient neurological rehabilitation settings. *Journal of Advanced Nursing, 59*(6), 612–622.

Wilson, D. B., Shayne, M., Lipsey, M., & Derzon, J. H. (1996, November). *Using indicators of the gap between need for service and available service capacity as the basis for needs assessment.* Paper presented at the annual meeting of the American Evaluation Association, Atlanta, GA.

Witkin, B. R., & Altschuld, J. W. (1995). *Planning and conducting needs assessment.* Thousand Oaks, CA: Sage.

Wulder, M. (2008). *Multivariate statistics: Data screening to assess validity/quality of input.* Retrieved August 13, 2009, from http://cfs.nrcan.gc.ca/subsite/wulder/screen

Index

analysis-related questions
for, 23–24 (table)
complex, working with,
21–22 (example)
dealing with, 15–25
sources of, problems in,
100–101 (table)
Quantitative data, 27–59
analysis, steps in, 58, 58 (table)
coping with, 27–58
problems in, summary of,
101–102 (table)
Quantitative information, 3

Regression, in needs assessment
data, 53
Rehabilitation Services Act, 55
Reliability, 46–47
Respondent characteristics, 36–37
Responses, weighting for
prioritization, 64–65

Sources, characteristics of,
29 (table)
Standard deviation, 40
Statistical significance, practical
aspects of, 57–58

Statistics
descriptive, 38–46
inferential, 36, 50–52
STEM (science, technology,
engineering, mathematics), 33, 47
Strategic planning
grid, 96 (figure)
linking prioritization to, 95–97
Summaries
collated across sources, 79–81
samples of, 76–81
steps, 74–76
Survey data, 78–79 (exhibit)
analysis, 28–29
Surveys, electronic, 30

Triple-scaling, 43 (table)
for competencies, 45 (table)
needs assessment survey,
42 (table)

Validity, 47–49
Variance, 40

Weighting responses, for
prioritization, 64–65
Within-methods approach, 2, 4, 51

Supporting researchers for more than 40 years

Research methods have always been at the core of SAGE's publishing program. Founder Sara Miller McCune published SAGE's first methods book, *Public Policy Evaluation*, in 1970. Soon after, she launched the *Quantitative Applications in the Social Sciences* series—affectionately known as the "little green books."

Always at the forefront of developing and supporting new approaches in methods, SAGE published early groundbreaking texts and journals in the fields of qualitative methods and evaluation.

Today, more than 40 years and two million little green books later, SAGE continues to push the boundaries with a growing list of more than 1,200 research methods books, journals, and reference works across the social, behavioral, and health sciences. Its imprints—Pine Forge Press, home of innovative textbooks in sociology, and Corwin, publisher of PreK–12 resources for teachers and administrators—broaden SAGE's range of offerings in methods. SAGE further extended its impact in 2008 when it acquired CQ Press and its best-selling and highly respected political science research methods list.

From qualitative, quantitative, and mixed methods to evaluation, SAGE is the essential resource for academics and practitioners looking for the latest methods by leading scholars.

For more information, visit **www.sagepub.com**.